The Best of Tokyo

The Best of
Tokyo

Revised and Updated

by
Don Morton
&
Naoko Tsunoi

Charles E. Tuttle Company
Rutland, Vermont & Tokyo, Japan

Photographs by Don Morton unless otherwise credited.
Additional information contributed by John Kennerdell.

Published by the Charles E. Tuttle Co., Inc.
of Rutland, Vermont & Tokyo, Japan
with editorial offices at
2-6 Suido 1-chome, Bunkyo-ku, Tokyo 112

Library of Congress Catalog Card No. 89-50660
International Standard Book No. 0-8048-1919-x

First edition, 1990
First revised edition, 1993
Second printing, 1995

Printed in Japan

Contents

We figure that if you ate three meals a day, each one in a different Tokyo restaurant, you'd finish sampling what the city has to offer by the year 2145, and you know they'd have opened some new places by then. Some say Tokyo is one of the world's best cities for dining. We are among them. Japanese . . 11 / Chinese . . 29 / Other Asian . . 33 / International . . 39 / General . . 46

For better or worse, Tokyo nearly floats on alcoholic beverages, be they imbibed for business reasons (a drink "after work" for most Japanese businessmen really means "as part of work"), social duty, or pleasure. Some people, of course, just hang out in bars to be cool.

What is modern Tokyo's raison d'être if not to spend? And there is no shortage of places to do so. Moreover, the variety of merchandise is truly astounding, as are the ways it is displayed. General Shops . . 67 / Traditional Shops . . 93 / Clothing . . 105

When Tokyo residents are not eating, drinking, or shopping, they're out and about visiting places. Tokyo does not lack for historical sites, museums, destinations for day jaunts, special views, or unique atmospheres, if you just know where to look.

Entertainment

Pity the soul so unimaginative as to claim to be bored in Tokyo, location of so many things to attend, participate in, listen to, watch, or dance to. Need we mention the fact that entertainment is one of Japan's main industries?

Services

Everyone needs a little help now and then—to find things, to do something better, or just to discover something new. Happily, there are many people and organizations that will answer questions about this city, often for free.

Sports

Whether you want to participate in a sport, or just watch, here are some hints to get you started. Remember that, this being Japan, you must purchase the entire outfit and paraphernalia before taking lesson number one.

Miscellaneous

Some things, like some people, don't fit into any particular category. Isn't that nice? And in a book such as this, these oddballs make for some of the best "bests." One could get the impression that Tokyo is a strange place to live.

Maps

Places outside of central Tokyo do not appear on the maps, but find everything else on these individual area guides: Roppongi . . 194 / Aoyama/Harajuku . . 196 / Shibuya . . 198 / Akasaka . . 199 / Shinjuku . . 200 / Asakusa . . 201 / Ginza . . 202

Index

Introduction

AH, TOKYO. A city of superlatives. And despite the occasional (and psychologically necessary) griping all rational foreigners indulge in, few will disagree that this city has been the scene of some very good times in our lives. Tokyo has been responsible for some of the best things we've ever tasted, seen, heard, bought, been unexpectedly delighted by, participated in, loved, or smiled at. (Are we gushing? To be fair, it also offers some of the worst things, like *natto*, but this will have to wait for another book.)

Here we present some of the "bests" this city has to offer. We've tried to point your way to some of the things you might not find in a saner guidebook, and to share our opinions on the most interesting of the things you might.

The Best of Tokyo is not meant to be a comprehensive guide, but it will point you toward the top restaurant/shop/arena/ neighborhood or whatever in a given category, and get you there straight away. In a city where the average tourist stays less than four days, this is a real plus. Even long-time residents may find in these pages things they never imagined existed. There could be incredible, life-changing discoveries waiting right around the corner.

By its very nature, any book on the best of anything is a book of opinions. These are ours. Note that "best" does not mean most expensive (and certainly not cheapest), nor does it always mean biggest, most quaintly Japanese, most well known, or even cutest. Readers should keep in mind the authors' motto throughout their research: "This book is meant to start arguments, not settle them."

One possible criticism we can foresee as we look through

what we've written is that a majority of places and things mentioned seem to be in the Roppongi, Shibuya, Aoyama, Ginza, Shinjuku, and Akasaka districts—areas not exactly off the beaten track. That's not our fault; good places are where you find them. Among the admittedly loose criteria we had in selecting any given "best" were accessibility, price, and a few intangibles, like maybe we just had a good time there one night.

The book is divided into sections—Eating, Drinking, Shopping, Places, Entertainment, Services, Sports, and the all-important Miscellaneous. Some places could be listed in more than one category; do you go to a bar, for example, to drink or to be entertained by the unique decor/music/fellow patrons? We hope this doesn't confuse you. It did us.

Note: *The official symbol of Tokyo is the ginkgo, a stylized leaf which is used on the title page and on other pages in this book. In autumn, its leaves turn yellow, and are greatly admired for their beauty.*

Eating

食物

JAPANESE

Best Sushi

SUSHISEI, Tsukiji, Roppongi, Akasaka, and other places. We know that trying to name the best sushi restaurant in Tokyo is like trying to name the best French restaurant in Paris. But read on. You don't need to be told that you can spend an awful lot of money in this city for good sushi. And some sushi restaurants, especially in the big hotels, get away with absolutely ludicrous prices using the excuse that if you want the freshest and the best raw fish, it has to cost a lot. Not so. You may need to arm yourself with a few Japanese words so that you can order at Sushisei, but that's not hard. The hearty *"Irasshaimase"* that greets you as you enter establishments large and small in this country is heartiest here, and the fish (and the ginger and the wasabi) the freshest. Best of all, you can usually eat like a king for about ¥3000 per person, and that includes a few beers or *tokkuri* of saké. Be prepared to wait, but do. Tsukiji, of course, is the site of Tokyo's huge fish market, and the sushi there may be a few minutes fresher. But the Roppongi and Akasaka locations have the best fellow diners: starlets on the arms of "producers," hipper-than-usual young Japanese (they don't giggle when foreigners try to talk to them), and, of course, other foreigners. See maps of respective areas.

4-13-9 Tsukiji, Chuo-ku. Hours: 8 a.m.–2 p.m., 5–9:30 p.m. Closed Sun. & hol. Tel: 3541-7720.

3-2-9 Nishi-Azabu, Minato-ku. Hours: 10:45 a.m.–2 p.m., 5–10 p.m. (Sun.: noon–2, 4:30–9:30 p.m.) Closed Wed. Tel: 3401-0578. *See Roppongi map.*

3-11-14 Akasaka, Minato-ku. Hours: 11:45 a.m.–2 p.m., 5–10:30 p.m. (Sat.: 4:45–10 p.m.) Closed Sun. & hol. Tel: 3582-9503. *See Akasaka map.*

GENROKUZUSHI, Harajuku. Given the delicate nature of raw fish, it may seem odd to recommend a conveyor-belt sushi place for anything but showing to a tourist friend. These Japanese fast-food joints offer good prices, but you get what you pay for. Sushi should be fresh, cut and assembled mere minutes before devouring. The trick to finding a good, cheap place in the conveyor-belt sushi category is to go to one that's crowded. It stands to reason that the more people there are eating, the fewer rotations each morsel will make, and the fresher it will be. Genrokuzushi is such a place. Situated on the stylish Omotesando "promenade" midway between the two pedestrian bridges, it sees a steady turnover of customers. And what not many foreigners know is that, even in a place like this, you can order your favorite from the sushi chef if you don't see it passing before you. Drawback: no beer or saké, probably to discourage lingering. But nevertheless, a good, quick, and cheap meal (you pay by the plate—¥120, ¥160, or ¥240, depending on the type of sushi).

5-8-5 Jingumae, Shibuya-ku. Hours: 11 a.m.–9 p.m. daily. Tel: 3498-3968. *See Aoyama/Harajuku map.*

Best Japanese Food Experience

KAISEKI refers to the delicate Japanese multi-course type of dining where each of eight or more seasonal treats complements the one going before and prepares the palate for the next. Everything is usually served on exquisite dishes that visually enhance the particular course they carry. It's the kind of meal everyone should have at least once in their lifetime, and once is probably all you would care to pay for; *kaiseki* makes all the other horror stories about the cost of eating in Tokyo pale in comparison. The best *kaiseki* places can run ¥40,000 per person or more, and introductions are sometimes necessary even to get in the door.

KISSO has always been a reliable place for good quality *kaiseki* in an atmosphere that is a mixture of modern and traditional. You can have it three ways: the counter seats about ten people, and whether you're by yourself or with others, this is our bet for the best place to sit, because it's entertaining to watch the chef (artist?) prepare the dishes. There's also a table area with soft lamps and paper partitions, or you can engage, for an extra charge of ¥1500, a private room for three to 20 people (the extra charge is ¥3000 for larger rooms). The lunch set, at ¥1200, is a real *kaiseki* bargain, and usually includes grilled fish, two simple assorted dishes like tofu or a veggie, rice, miso and pickles. You can also have one of the *o-bento*, at ¥1700 and ¥2500, or one of the larger *kaiseki* courses for ¥3800–¥5000. Dinner courses start at ¥8000, and we recommend the Chef Choice course, leaving it to the chef to select which seasonal delicacies you will eat.

B1 AXIS Bldg., 5-17-1 Roppongi, Minato-ku. Hours: 11:30 a.m.–2 p.m., 5:30–9 p.m. Closed Sun. Tel: 3582-4191. See Roppongi map.

But perhaps you think *kaiseki* should be a bit fancier. Then by all means visit **JISAKU** on the scenic Sumida over in Tsukiji, which has been serving *kaiseki* in superb surroundings since the Edo period. It's a huge, two-story

house with about 30 rooms, capable of accommodating parties ranging from three to 100 people, and each room has a view of their beautiful garden and pond. In addition to *kaiseki,* Jisaku offers *shabu shabu* and *sukiyaki*. A specialty is *mizutaki,* chicken broth with seasonal delicacies. Lunches start at ¥8000, dinner at ¥15,000. Expect also to pay for drinks, 10-percent service charge (20 percent at dinner) two different three-percent taxes and a ¥500 table charge. We didn't say it was cheap. There's a "ladies' menu" whereby women in groups of more than four can lunch for ¥6000–¥8000, including taxes, service, and table charges.

14-19 Akashicho, Chuo-ku. Hours: noon–10 p.m. daily. Tel: 3541-2391. *Five-minute walk from Tsukiji Station.*

Another good *kaiseki* place, again in Roppongi, is **O-AN**. On the second floor, but reached by its own outside stairway, O-an has no tables or chairs, only private tatami rooms, from six to 28 mats in size. Lunch *kaiseki* (eight dishes) goes for ¥7000 (figuring out to ¥8700 after tax and a service charge have been added). Dinners (ten dishes) can be had for about ¥18,000, including drinks. And for a mere ¥50,000 you get a "companion," English-speaking if you wish, to serve your dishes and pour your saké. It's only money.

6-1-12 Roppongi, Minato-ku. Hours: noon–3:30, 5–11 p.m., (until 9 p.m. on Sun. & hol.). Tel: 3479-0023. See Roppongi map.

Best Sashimi

UOSAN could be referred to as a drinking place, since most customers order their sashimi to go with their saké. The sashimi is not the best, but the freshness, variety, and low price are unequalled. The two top stories are tatami rooms, but it is the two counter-seating rooms below that are popular with the blue-collar clientele of the down-town Monzen-Nakacho area. It opens at 4 p.m., but people start lining up 30 minutes earlier, and most of them seem to know each other. Many have been going there for more than 25 years. By 5, the counter areas will be full and bustling with as many as 50 people in an area that measures less than 10 tatami mats. The walls are crowded with more than 150 menu items, with prices starting at ¥50. Most sashimi dishes are between ¥200 and ¥300, about half of what most restaurants charge, but the portions are twice as big! The best thing to do is get there at 4, at the latest, 5. Make a day of it by visiting the

Tomioka Hachimangu Shrine to admire their display of valuable *mikoshi* (portable shrines used in festivals), wander around the old streets with their many traditional confectioneries, or stop by the Tomioka Fudosan to see its collection of art and religious statues. Both are across the street from Uosan.

1-5-4 Tomioka, Koto-ku. Hours: 4–10 p.m. Closed Sun & hol. Tel: 3461-8071.

Best Soba

As the name implies, **TACHIGUI SOBA** is where you eat while standing up. These places are everywhere, sometimes even on train platforms. Don't be frightened by the bestial slurping sounds that emerge from them, they're the best places to stop in to when you're short of time (and money—they're very cheap). You can have your order up in about a minute. Order the *kakesoba*, which is plain *soba* in a broth, the *wakame,* with seaweed, or tempura. Prices are in the ¥250–¥450 range.

Best Tofu Restaurant

GOEMON in Hakusan pays homage to the humble soybean curd, elevating it almost to *kaiseki* elegance. The place itself is in a beautiful Japanese house, but it is possible to reserve outdoor huts and dine by a little waterfall if you should so choose. All of the tofu served is homemade, and it's best to go with one of the sets, priced from ¥5000 to ¥7000, which change with the seasons.

1-1-26 Hon-Komagome. Hours: 5–10 p.m. (3–8 p.m. Sun. & hol.) Closed Mon. Tel: 3811-2015.

Best-Named Restaurant

KUIMONOYA RAKU, Roppongi & Harajuku. It means "a fun place to eat," and just a look in the door will confirm the truth in the name. There are no English menus, but all the food, which is Japanese (some Chinese), is on the counter for your inspection, so you can just point to what you want if necessary.

7-14-2 Roppongi, Minato-ku. Hours: 5:30–11:30 p.m. daily. Tel: 3403-0869. *See Roppongi map.*

Yoshino Bldg. 4-31-6 Jingumae, Shibuya-ku. Hours: 6 p.m.–midnight. Closed Sun. Tel: 3423-3759. *See Aoyama/Harajuku map.*

Best Grilled Fish

TAMAKYU, Shibuya. Grilled fish was never better than at this funky little place that makes a dent in the huge 109 Department Store. Melt-in-your-mouth fare complemented by some great sakés, hot and cold. Only for serious eaters. See Miscellaneous section for more on this place and its history.

2-30-4 Dogenzaka, Shibuya-ku. Hours: 4–10:30 p.m. Closed Sun. & hol. Tel: 3461-4803. See Shibuya map.

Best "We Love Nature" Dinner

UKAI TORIYAMA, Takao. It's more like a village that cooks than a restaurant, this peaceful place in the hills of Takao. That's at the end of the Chuo Line (take the express) out of Tokyo or Shinjuku stations, and also at the end of the Keio Line out of Shinjuku. Shuttle buses run from both stations to the restaurant/village. Each village hut contains a charcoal grill or two or more, for you to cook the skewered things, such as chicken, eggplant, onion, mushroom, etc. that are brought out to you. It's a fine place for revelry (and a great Japan experience) since all guests are provided with inhibition-suppressing *yukata*, light summer kimono. Or you could just sip your saké and gaze introspectively at the verdant surroundings. Meditate on the sound of the little creek that passes through the village, and make up a few *haiku*. Telephones in each hut facilitate ordering those three more bottles of Japan's good brew or some more of those yummy sparrows.

3426 Minami-Asakawacho, Hachioji. Hours: 11 a.m.–8 p.m., until 7 p.m. on Sun. & hol. Tel: 0426-61-0739.

Best Tempura

TSUNAHACHI SHINJUKU has many branches all over town, but the Shinjuku store has the feeling of returning to the original. The building itself, with its stone floor and wooden chairs, brings back a turn-of-the-century feeling. It's lively and noisy like a good sushi bar, but the food is the main attraction. Tempura is fried right in front of you and served right away. Prices are reasonable: ¥1100 for six kinds, ¥1800 for eight, including rice, soup, and pickles. Lunch and dinner menus are the same.

3-31-8 Shinjuku, Shinjuku-ku. Hours: 11 a.m.–10 p.m. daily. Tel: 3352-1012. *See Shinjuku map.*

Best Cook-Your-Own Yakitoriya

HAYASHI, Ginza and Akasaka. Leave Tokyo for a gentler place. All the interior furnishings, including the support columns and the ceiling itself, were brought here from Takayama, a village in the Japan Alps noted for its woodworking and architectural skills. The charcoal fireplaces are of the type you would find in that area of the country. Choose your *yakitori* and cook it yourself over a charcoal grill. At the Akasaka branch you still cook your own but order the *yakitori* from a menu. A perfect place to take your visiting friends for that requisite traditional Japanese dinner.

5-10-6 Ginza, Chuo-ku. Hours: 11:30 a.m.–2 p.m., 5–10:30 p.m. Closed Sun. & hol. Tel: 3572-4584. *See Ginza map.*

Sanno Kaikan 4F. 2-14-1 Akasaka, Minato-ku. Hours: 11:30 a.m.–1:30 p.m., 5:30–11 p.m. Closed Sun. & hol. Tel: 3582-4078. *See Akasaka map.*

Best Outdoor Yakitori

UNDER THE TRACKS, Yurakucho. Sometimes the experience of eating in a place is more important than the food being eaten, and that's the case at any of these little *yakitoriya*, restaurants specializing in grilled chicken and vegetables on skewers, under the tracks in Yurakucho/ Hibiya. There's a feeling here that time stopped sometime around 1949, and the attitude is definitely working-class. This is gruff old Tokyo—or at least what's left of it in the slick Ginza district. The places don't exist during the day, but at night they appear, makeshift tables with overturned beer crates for seats. Your order is taken by a gruff but probably friendly guy after he brings you the beer or saké you have ordered. There are all sorts of things on skewers besides chicken, but if you just order *yakitori,* you'll get white chicken. Also available, of course, are things like chicken hearts (*hatsu*), minced chicken (*tsukune*), liver (*reba*), wings (*teba*), etc. The area is by the Tourist Information Center in Yurakucho. See Ginza map.

Best Oden

Oden is the Japanese stew made of vegetables, fish cakes, eggs, and tofu simmered for hours in a broth. This dish is popular in the winter and can be had at various restaurants, street stalls, and even convenience stores. Many people pick some up along with a bit of warm saké on the way home from work on a cold day. Ginza's **OTAKO** has been serving up its own *oden* for more than 60 years. They have an English menu explaining what each ingredient is, but you may want to forego that.

8-6-19 Ginza, Chuo-ku. Hours: 4 p.m.–1 a.m. Closed Sun. & hol. Tel: 3571-0751. See Ginza map.

Best Unagi

NODAIWA, in Higashi-Azabu, has been serving eel since the Edo period, so they must be doing something right. Sweet-tasting and tender, *unagi* is one Japanese dish that goes well with wine. And you can sit at a table or go native in a tatami room. Meals start at ¥2500.

1-5-4 Higashi-Azabu, Minato-ku. Hours: 11 a.m.–1:30 p.m., 5–7:30 p.m. Closed Sun. & hol. Tel: 3583-7852. See Roppongi map.

Best Kushiage

Incredibly delicious things deep-fried on skewers. **HANTEI**, in Nezu, is a place that does what they do very well. Located in a beautiful three-story traditional wooden house near Ueno Park, it's a comfortable and proper place to enjoy all the skewered things that make up *kushiage*. Ordering "the course" (¥2500) will get you a vegetable, six skewers of *kushiage* (prawns, chicken, beef, mushrooms, asparagus, potatoes, and things like that), and two small appetizers. An additional six skewers will cost you

¥1200. Near the end of your meal, the chef will ask if you prefer rice or noodles to top off your meal. You can't go wrong with either. The first floor contains a rectangular counter and some tables, the second has small tatami rooms that can be reserved for groups.

2-12-15 Nezu, Bunkyo-ku. Hours: 5–10 p.m. (4–9 p.m. on hol.). Closed Sun. & 3rd Mon. Tel: 3828-1440.

Best Udon

TORIJAYA is a Kansai-style restaurant in the old *geisha* quarter of Kagurazaka. The area was one of the few spared in the firebombing during WW II, and makes a great stroll for a feeling of what Tokyo used to look like. Torijaya has long occupied this site, but is now on the ground floor of a new building. Inside it retains its traditional Japanese style, with stone floors and small booths or rooms divided by paper partitions. But the main attraction is the *udon-suki*. This is a *nabe*-style (pot) dish with big, uneven noodles a centimeter in diameter, simmering in a delicious broth along with about 14 other ingredients, like chicken, shrimp, clams, and vegetables. For ¥1400 you get just this. The lunch set, for ¥2500, includes other small dishes like sashimi, seasonal specialties, and a bit of fruit to top it off. Order the *udon kaiseki* course at dinnertime, comprising nine dishes, such as sashimi, tempura, cooked veggies, and other seasonal delicacies in addition to the *udon-suki* for ¥5500. From the McDonald's at Iidabashi Station, walk away from the river until you see a temple on the left. Torijaya is across the street on the corner.

4-2 Kagurazaka, Shinjuku-ku. Hours: 11:30 a.m.–10:30 p.m. daily. Tel: 3260-6661.

Best Udon Entertainment

The *udon* at **USAGIYA** is pretty good, but the main attraction here is watching it being prepared. All but lost in the glitz of Roppongi Crossing, this basement place has only five tables and a counter. Make sure you sit at the eight-seat counter in the back to see the chef in action.

B1 Rokuei Bldg., 7-14-11 Roppongi, Minato-ku. Hours: 11 a.m.–4 a.m. (until 11 p.m. on Sun & hol.) Tel: 3401-6208. See Roppongi map.

Best Shabu-shabu

Shabu-shabu is the fun dinner where you briefly swirl thinly sliced beef through a vat of boiling soup stock at your table (making, it is presumed, a sound like "shabu-shabu"). There are hundreds of *shabu-shabu* restaurants in Tokyo. **HASSAN** (Roppongi 3403-8333, Shibuya 3464-8883) and **SHABUZEN** (Roppongi 3585-5388) are notable. These places usually offer "all you can eat" courses for around ¥5000–¥10,000. But for the best combination of atmosphere, service, taste, and price, it's the **ZAKURO** chain. They're all easy to get to; one is across from the American Embassy, another is in the basement of the TBS Building in Akasaka, and a third is near the main Ginza intersection.

Nihon Jitensha Kaikan B1. 1-9-15 Akasaka, Minato-ku. Hours: 11 a.m.–10 p.m. Tel: 3582-2661.

Akasaka TBS Kaikan B1. 5-3-3 Akasaka, Minato-ku. Hours: 11 a.m.–10 p.m. Tel: 3582-6841. See Akasaka map.

Ginza Sanwa Bldg. B1. 4-6-1 Ginza, Chuo-ku. Hours: 11 a.m.–9 p.m. Tel: 3535-4421. See Ginza map.

Best Robatayaki

INAKAYA, Roppongi & Akasaka. *Robatayaki* refers to eating while sitting around a fireplace. Inakaya is a favorite place of many Tokyoites to take visitors from abroad, as it's a memorable Japanese eating experience. Two chefs are seated in the middle of a sea of food, and they shout a welcome to you, shout the names of everything you order, and then shout you out when you leave. Noisy place, Inakaya. A visit here is best enjoyed, we have found, when someone else is paying for it, as meals can pass the ¥10,000 per person mark before you know it. Fun, though.

7-8-4 Roppongi, Minato-ku. Hours: 5 p.m.–5 a.m. Tel: 3405-9866. *See Roppongi map.*

3-12-7 Akasaka, Minato-ku. Hours: 5–11 p.m. Tel: 3586-3054. *See Akasaka map.*

If Inakaya is a bit too dear for your battle-weary wallet, try **MUSASHI** in the SL (Steam Locomotive) drinking district around Shimbashi Station. The system is the same as fancier places, but a sign outside claims that every dish is only ¥280. A pair of people, unless they're very big eaters/drinkers, can get out of there for under ¥5000. It's nice not to be dependent on being able to read the menu, as everything is on display just waiting for your pointing finger.

2-9-17 Shimbashi, Minato-ku. Hours: 5–10:40 p.m. Closed Sun & hol. Tel: 3580-3550. *Three minutes from Shimbashi Station.*

Best Tonkatsu

Tonkatsu (deep-fried pork cutlet) restaurants are easy to spot for their plastic menus and sheer number; there must be at least three near even the smallest train station. But the difference at **KATSUKICHI** becomes apparent right at the door. There is no display case, just a big wooden sign and a blue-and-white *noren*, making it look a bit like an *izakaya*. At the bottom of the stairs you go through a huge wooden door, making you feel as though you are entering a daimyo's castle. Inside, the Japanese pottery on display further dispels the image of the average *tonkatsu* restaurant. Dishes start at ¥1400 for both lunch and dinner, and they have a large selection to choose from. Even a meatless version. Have the all-you-can-eat salad, offering about seven kinds of vegetable served on a big platter.

B1 KDD Bldg., 3-9-10 Shibuya, Shibuya-ku. Hours: 11:30 a.m.–2:30 p.m., 5–10 p.m. daily. Tel: 5485-1123. *See Shibuya map.*

Best Old-Tokyo Dinner Date

KANDA "TRIANGLE ZONE" The streets here have survived Tokyo's various bombings and earthquakes. This is the part of Kanda where the streets form a triangle, and the area is referred to as such. Each restaurant has its own special character, and all are in wooden Japanese houses over 50 years old, some 100 or more.

Start the evening with a light serving of cold soba at **YABU SOBA** (2-10 Awajicho, Kanda, Chiyoda-ku. Hours: 11:30 a.m.–7 p.m. Closed Mon. Tel: 3251-0287). The place has a beautiful garden and is in a house that is an antique in itself. Start with saké and a few small dishes and move on to your choice of *soba*. And more saké. Then decide whether you want fish or chicken for your main course and head for one of the following:

BOTAN (1-15 Sudacho, Kanda, Chiyoda-ku. Hours: noon–8 p.m. Closed Sun. & hol. Tel: 3251-0577) offers only chicken *sukiyaki torisuki,* served in steel pots and cooked over a charcoal fire (*ryokan* style) in little rooms. Only charcoal is used—no gas. Botan uses only range-fed chickens. Since there's only one course, which at ¥5800 includes rice, pickles, and fruit, non-speakers of Japanese will have no problem. You will be taken to a room (sometimes shared with other diners) where you are served without being asked by waitresses, some on the far side of 70.

If you opt for the fish, direct your steps to **ISEGEN** (1-11-1 Sudacho, Kanda, Chiyoda-ku. Hours: 11:30 a.m.–2 p.m., 4–9 p.m. Closed Sun. Tel: 3251-1229). The specialty here is *anko,* (angler fish or monk fish), which is served in a stew called, appropriately enough, *anko-nabe*—a pot of *anko.* The best time to eat *anko* is September through April.

And wind up your progressive meal with a delicious-at-this-place (usually questionable elsewhere) Japanese sweet at **TAKEMURA** (1-19 Sudacho, Kanda, Chiyoda-ku. Hours: 11 a.m.–8 p.m. Closed Sun. & hol. Tel: 3251-2328).

CHINESE

Best Chinese Food Selection

TOKYO DAIHANTEN, Shinjuku, at about six floors, is Japan's biggest Chinese restaurant. Szechwan, Cantonese, Peking style—all kinds of Chinese food are available here. The 3rd floor is where you'll find the *dim sum*, served Hong Kong style, in carts rolled around to your table. They offer about 30 kinds of *dim sum*, about half of them Chinese sweets, at about ¥600 each. Traditionally a lunch meal, it's served here all day long, but if you don't get there before 8, it may be all gone.

5-17-13 Shinjuku, Shinjuku-ku. Hours: 11 a.m.–10 p.m. Open daily. Tel: 3202-0121. *See Shinjuku map.*

But biggest is not necessarily best, and some of these smaller Chinese places may do their specialty best. Read on.

Best Szechwan

RYUNOKO, Harajuku. Tiny place serving up great, spicy Szechwan dishes. Try the tasting course if you're not sure what you want. Cooking classes are available on the second Saturday of the month, at 2:30 p.m., for ¥3500. And you can eat what you cook; how can you lose?

1-8-5 Jingumae, Shibuya-ku. Hours: 11:30 a.m.–3 p.m., 5–9:30 p.m., until 9 p.m. on Sun & hol. Open daily. Tel: 3402-9419. *See Aoyama/Harajuku map.*

29

Best Designer Chinese

TONG FU, Roppongi, and **TONG FU WEST**, Aoyama. If you think "designer" is an odd category for restaurants, then you haven't been here very long. And you certainly haven't been to Tong Fu. The slick bar at Tong Fu, Roppongi, is a good place to rendezvous, especially if you are meeting a group of people—there's a small private room for drinks and an outdoor area that's quite pleasant.

6-7-11 Roppongi, Minato-ku. Hours: 11:30 a.m.–2 p.m., 5 p.m.–3:30 a.m. Closed Sun. Tel: 3403-3527. *See Roppongi map.*

2-29 Minami-Aoyama, Minato-ku. Hours: noon–3 p.m. 6 p.m.–4:30 a.m. (5–11:30 p.m. on Sun.) Tel: 3479-1067. *See Aoyama/Harajuku map.*

Best Peking Duck

Beijing Duck? **ZUIEN BEKKAN**, Shinjuku. Very Chinese utilitarian atmosphere, the proprietor a gruff old Chinese guy who treats you in a traditional Chinese manner—he orders you to wait, or tells you to squeeze in with someone else at a table, or kicks you out when he thinks you're finished if there's someone else waiting. Anyway, the duck comes as three dishes—duck skin wrapped in thin pastries, duck meat cooked with vegetables, and duck bone soup. Enough for three people and all for ¥7000. Other Beijing-style dishes, like *sui-gyoza*, steamed dumplings, are good, too.

1-10-6 Shinjuku, Shinjuku-ku. Hours: 11 a.m.–10 p.m. Tel: 3351-3511. See Shinjuku map.

Best Taiwanese

TAINAN TAMI. No-frills, authentic Taiwanese food cooked by authentic Taiwanese people. Pork ears—also knuckles, guts, and kidneys—and good noodles. Very cheap—¥150 and up. Crowded, but worth waiting for.

2-45-1 Kabukicho, Shinjuku-ku. Hours: 11:30 a.m.–2:30 p.m., 5 p.m.–4 a.m. Tel: 3232-8839. See Shinjuku map.

Chiba Building 1F. 3-10-7 Roppongi, Minato-ku. Hours: 11 a.m.–2 p.m., 5 p.m.–2 a.m. Tel: 3408-2111. See Roppongi map.

1-17-6 Dogenzaka, Shibuya-ku. Hours: 11 a.m.–2 p.m., 5 p.m.–2 a.m. Tel: 3464-7544. See Shibuya map.

2-1-13 Nishi-Kanda, Chiyoda-ku. Hours: 11 a.m.–2 p.m., 5–11 p.m. Tel: 3263-4530.

Best Chinese Vegetarian

BODAIJU, Shiba. The menu is complete. Peking duck, beef, and pork dishes—the works. But after a full Chinese meal here, you will not have eaten anything but vegetables although they taste like meat. Nothing, as one veggie wag once said, that had a mother. For Bodaiju is a painless vegetarian restaurant for vegetarians who don't like vegetables unless they taste like meat. The edibles are free of MSG as well.

Bukkyo Dendo Center, 4-3-14 Shiba, Minato-ku. Hours: 11:30 a.m.–2:30 p.m., 5:30–8 p.m. Closed Sun. & hol. Tel: 3456-3257.

OTHER ASIAN

Best Thai Food

BAN-THAI, Shinjuku and Futako Tamagawa. There seems to have been a proliferation of Thai restaurants in Tokyo recently, and most of them are pretty good. Some offer fiery hot fare, others are a bit Japanized. But Ban-Thai, with its street-stall delicious fried rice and its college-student Thai waiters and waitresses, wins the honors for most authentic. The menu, in English, is coded with red dots to indicate spiciness, and of course masochistic types can request extra chilies. The beef salad and the lemon-grass-flavored soups are especially good. The Shinjuku branch is set in the seediest of Shinjuku neighborhoods, Kabukicho, amid touchy-feelie places and raucous strip joints. Try to get there early on Friday or Saturday nights.

1-23-14 Kabukicho, Shinjuku-ku. Hours: 5 p.m.–1 a.m. Sat. & Sun., 11:30 a.m.–11 p.m. weekdays. Tel: 3207-0068. See Shinjuku map.

1-15-1 Tamagawa, Setagaya-ku. Hours: 11:30 a.m.–3 p.m., 5–10 p.m. (11:30 a.m.–10 p.m. Sat., Sun., & hol.) Tel: 5716-5697.

For "designer" Thai food, try **CAY**, Aoyama, Spiral Building basement. More a fashion spot than an authentic restaurant, but nonetheless a good night out. Cay is sometimes turned into an evening concert hall for live music that ranges from R&B to new wave to often great ethnic sounds. Check *Pia* or *Tokyo Journal's CityScope* to see what's on.

5-6-23 Minami-Aoyama, Minato-ku. Hours: 6 p.m.–10:30. Closed Sun. & hol. Tel: 3498-5790. *See Aoyama/Harajuku map.*

Best Indian Food

MOTI (not "Moti's"), Roppongi. As soon as a new Indian place opens, Indian food aficionados descend on it to try it out, and their conversations are predictable. "How's the *alu gobi*?" "Pretty good, but Moti's has more cauliflower, and this *nan* is too heavy." In addition to great food (our favorite: chicken *tikka masala*), Moti is

pleasant, the service fast, and the prices reasonable. What more could you ask for in a restaurant? It's the kind of place you miss when you're traveling outside of Japan. None of this is a secret, of course, and there is always a wait at lunch and dinner time at the Roppongi branches. But a leisurely lunch after 2 p.m. or early dinner before 6 p.m. will get you around the crowds. Otherwise, it's worth the wait, and the beautiful-people watching is hard to beat. Moti's ongoing popularity has spawned additional branches, and there are now five in central Tokyo, two each in Roppongi and Akasaka, and one in Kichijoji. Open every day, and that means every day, even New Year's.

Hama Bldg. 3F. 6-2-35 Roppongi, Minato-ku. Hours: 11:30 a.m.–10 p.m. Tel: 3479-1939. See Roppongi map.

Roppongi Plaza 3F, 3-12-6 Roppongi, Minato-ku. Hours: 11:30 a.m.–1 a.m. (until 10 on Sun. & Hol.) Tel: 5410-6871. See Roppongi map.

Akasaka Floral Bldg. 2F. 3-8-8 Akasaka, Minato-ku. Hours: 11:30 a.m.–10 p.m. daily. Tel: 3582-3620. See Akasaka map.

Kinpa Bldg. 3F. 2-14-31 Akasaka, Minato-ku. Hours: 11:30 a.m.–10 p.m. Tel: 3584-6640. See Akasaka map.

85 Tokyo Bldg., B1, 1-8-10 Honcho, Kichijoji, Musashino-shi. Hours: 11:30 a.m.–10 p.m. daily. Tel: 0422-21-7010.

Best Indonesian Food

BENGAWAN SOLO, Roppongi, is a great place for a large party to dine together, the long tables in the back room facilitating the seating of groups as large as you like. And it's just as appropriate for lunch for two. Try the

Bengawan Solo lunch, a mixture of six or seven dishes all served on rice with a stick of *satay*, Indonesian for *yakitori*. Sort of a sampler of the restaurant's fare. You also get soup and brewed-in-the-cup Indonesian coffee (flavorful and easy on the stomach), and some killer chili sauce. The food is consistently delicious and exciting, the service swift, and the prices very reasonable. An old Tokyo favorite.

7-18-13 Roppongi, Minato-ku. Hours: 11:30 a.m.–2:30 p.m., 5–9:45 p.m. daily. Tel: 3403-3031. *See Roppongi map.*

Also very good in the Shibuya area is **JEMBATAN MERRAH**, where owner Nagahama offers a monthly chef's recommendation using seasonal ingredients imported directly from Indonesia, some of which cannot be found in other Tokyo Indonesian restaurants. It's quite large without looking so, occupying the upper three floors of a four-story building, each able to accommodate about 25 people. The fourth floor sports a bar and some tables, making it a good place to have a small party. It's a stone's throw from Tokyu Bunkamura and a convenient place to stop by either before or after a film or concert.

1-3 Maruyamacho, Shibuya-ku. Hours: 11:30 a.m.–midnight, daily. Tel: 3476-6424. *See Shibuya map.*

Best Balinese Food

WARUNG 1, Shibuya. Managing to be ethnic and stylish at the same time, Warung 1 is also a haven from squealing, giggling, youthful Shibuya. For some reason, the hordes of teeny-boppers eschew this little place, and the clientele is mostly Japanese adult-hip. Almost anything on the big menu is tasty, and there's a good selection of Southeast

Asian beers. The fruit salad is recommended, as are the straight-up margaritas.

Saito Daini Bldg. 2-29-18 Dogenzaka, Shibuya-ku. Hours: 5:30–10:30 p.m. (until 11:50 for drinks) daily. Tel: 3464-9795. *See Shibuya map.*

Best Cambodian Food

ANGKOR WAT, Yoyogi. Established and still run by Cambodian refugees. Started in a former sushi shop, it gained popularity and expanded fourfold. But there are still lines at mealtimes, so try to arrive either early or late to avoid the crush.

1-38-13 Yoyogi, Shibuya-ku. Hours: 11 a.m.–2 p.m., 5–10 p.m. daily, but no lunch on Sun. & hol. Tel: 3370-3019.

Best Yakiniku

TOKAI-EN, Shinjuku. When you want the best (and the cheapest) of anything, go to the specialists. They've been in business for more than 23 years. If you're new in town and not familiar with Korean barbecue, this is the kind of food you usually cook by yourself at your table: marinated beef and other meats, vegetables, and many other yummy items, spiced up if you wish by the indispensable *kimchi*, the fiery and garlicky cabbage (or radish or cucumber) Korean condiment. The 26-dish "viking" (that's what the Japanese call smorgasbord) on the 6th floor is a great deal for ¥2800. You sit on tatami mats and it's kind of greasy, and you are not served top cuts, but you *can* eat a lot. The 1st and 2nd floors are open until 3 a.m. The 7th and 8th floors feature private tatami rooms.

1-6-3 Kabukicho, Shinjuku-ku. Hours: 6F, 7F, 8F: 5–10:30 p.m. (from 11 a.m. on weekends) daily. 1F, 2F: 11 a.m.–4 a.m. Tel: 3205-1292. See Shinjuku map.

Azabu Juban, with its more than 20 *yakiniku* places of various types, from wooden, one-story huts to modern, multi-storied restaurants, is Tokyo's Korean barbecue quarter. Look along Sakurada-Dori for several good places, including the well-known Korean home-cooking place, Kusa-no-ie, that serves rice chicken soup in addition to grilled meats. Some others are located in the vicinity of the Korean Embassy along Sendai-zaka.

Best Nepalese

KANTIPUR, in Shibuya and Roppongi, serves up some Nepalese specialties like the delicious steamed dumplings called *momo*, curries, and Tibetan noodles. Stars on the menu indicate degree of spiciness. Drinks? Sure. How about a Fish Tail Fizz? Or a Kathmandu Lady?

Roppongi Fuji Bldg., 2F. 3-2-6 Nishi Azabu, Minato-ku. Hours: 11:30 a.m.–11 p.m. daily. Lunch sets available (except Sunday) until 4 p.m. See Roppongi map.

Shibuya: Sunrise Sakuragaoka Bldg., Shibuya-ku. Hours: 11:30 –3 p.m. Tel: 3770-5358. See Shibuya map.

INTERNATIONAL

Best Food Street

THE LITTLE STREET that runs from Kichijoji Station (starts near Marui) to Inokashira Park. Word is that it became what it is while trying to attract the young generation and young families walking to or from the park, and it now sports more than ten stores and restaurants offering goods and goodies from Thailand, India, the Philippines, Vietnam, Indonesia, etc. Among these is the long-established Rauya, a live music venue that also serves various curries, teas, and coffees (see entertainment section for music information). The street is a great place to browse for clothes from India or Indonesia, perhaps a drum from Thailand, or a coffee or beer at the bistro of your choice. At the Inokashira Park end there is a little *yakitoriya* called Isegen, where you can order and eat your *yakitori* while standing at the outdoor counter. Mellow, friendly street, this.

Best Spanish

The thing to order at **SABADO SABADETE** is paella, which is prepared in a one-meter pan and served up at around 8:30 or 9 p.m., usually to applause. The open kitchen, Spanish family atmosphere, and some very good sangria and other dishes make this *restaurante* a fun and festive place.

2F Genteel Shiroganedai, 5-3-2 Shiroganedai, Minato-ku. Hours: 6–11 p.m. Closed Sun. Tel: 3445-9353/63.

Best French Restaurant

You can't swing a *chat mort* in this city without hitting another new and trendy French restaurant, and trying to choose the best one is only slightly less dumb than trying to choose the best Japanese place. But that never stopped us. We like **BRASSERIE BARNARD** at the Institut Franco-Japonais in Ichigaya, operated by the reliable restaurant of the same name in Roppongi. Adjacent to a modest lawn, it has only about 10 tables, but this will double when the weather is good and more tables are set up on the covered terrace. It's slightly careworn, bringing to mind a country, home-style eatery rather than a swanky Parisian bistro. And stress is placed on taste rather than presentation. Best of all, prices are reasonable, with lunches at ¥1350 and ¥2000 and special dinner courses starting at ¥3500. Bon apetit.

15 Funagawaracho, Ichigaya, Shinjuku-ku. Hours: noon–2 p.m., 6–9:30 p.m. Closed Sun & hol. Tel: 3260-9639.

Best Latin American Restaurant

EL MOCAMBO in Nishi-Azabu is always a good time. Dishes and drinks from a dozen countries from Mexico to Chile, a great, open interior and the apparent fun being had by the waiters and waitresses from as many countries make this a good place for gatherings of any size. You could have Brazilian potatoes served by a Peruvian person, or tacos offered by an Argentine. You get the picture.

1-4-38 Nishi-Azabu, Minato-ku. Hours: 6 p.m.–midnight (until 2 a.m. on Fri. & Sat.). Closed Sun. Tel: 5410-0468. *See Roppongi map.*

Best Mexican Restaurant

There's been a rash of Mexican opening lately, but for atmosphere, variety, and quality, we opt for **LA ESCONDIDA** in Nishi-Azabu. Open and spacious for a basement place, this is simply a good, if a bit pricey, place to enjoy dishes from all over Mexico, not just Mexican-American fare. You can request tunes from the roving mariachi trio, or then you might want to request that they play on the other side of the room. Seems like there are about three birthdays celebrated there every time we go.

2-24-12 Nishi-Azabu, Minato-ku. Hours: 5 p.m.–midnight (1–4 p.m. on Sun.). Tel: 3486-0330. *See Roppongi map.*

Best Ethiopian

Not that there's a lot of competition, but **QUEEN SHEEBA** in Nakameguro is a cozy and friendly place offering three courses, for between ¥4000 and ¥6000. The ¥4000 course, for example, includes samosa, salad, egg with beef, and either beef, chicken, or lamb stew. Also beans & lamb and two kinds of bread.

B1 New Age Higashiyama, Shibuya-ku. Hours: 5:30–10:30 p.m. daily. Tel: 3794-1801.

Best Italian Restaurant

Jeez, who can pick the best of the hundreds of great Italian places in this city? Well, since this is an "opinion-ated" guide to this city, we can, that's who. An Italian restaurant, in our opinion, should offer Italian foods, Italian wines, breads, spices and all that, but most of all it has to offer an Italian attitude. And the Japanese, no matter how long they study cooking in Rome, Florence or Palermo, no matter how well they learn the Italian language or culture (sound familiar?) will never, never be Italian. So the reason why **SORRISO** in Iidabashi is our bet for best place in this category is that it is run by an Italian's Italian named Angelo, who, dressed in soiled whites, greets you, seats you and feeds you like he's your mama, all the while displaying an ear-to-ear grin. Angelo is cool. Put yourself in his hands and eat and drink everything he recommends. Can't go wrong. The place itself is a combination of modern and rustic and just a bit too large, but, hey, whatsamatta you? You want perfection? From exit B4b of Iidabashi subway station, go right for about 50 meters, you'll see it.

3-1-15 Kagurazaka, Shinjuku-ku. Hours: noon–2 p.m., 6–10 p.m. Closed Sun. Tel: 3235-4477.

Best Russian Restaurants

The fare at **URAL**, in Nishi-Azabu, is home cooking, Russian style. And while the food is hearty and tasty, the main enticement of Ural is the "home." When you enter, you feel that you've arrived at a dinner party in the home of a nice Russian lady. And that's not too far wrong. Mrs. Shvets sees to it that the homey atmosphere prevails throughout the meal, especially if you dine in one of the small upstairs dining rooms of this lovely old Western-style house. Sets from ¥5000 to ¥7000 are best. Try the *piroshki* as well. Reservations required.

1-9-7 Nishi-Azabu, Minato-ku. Hours: 6–9 p.m. Closed Sun. & hol., all of July and August. Tel: 3403-1703. *See Roppongi map.*

Less homey (unless you live in a crypt) but an unforget-table dining experience is **VOLGA** in Kamiyacho, near Tokyo Tower. Some interior designer pushed the enve-lope beyond the superficiality you may sense in some Tokyo eateries, where form rules over function. How to describe a meal here? Perhaps like dining in the basement of St. Basil's Cathedral prior to 1917. It's seedy, plush, gloomy, and fascinating.

3-5-14 Shiba Koen, Minato-ku. Hours: 11:30 a.m.–2:30 p.m., 5–9:30 p.m. Closed Mon. Tel: 3433-1766. *See Roppongi map.*

Best American Food

ROKKO GRILL, Aoyama Itchome. A marriage between an American diner and a Japanese beanery, this place will seat only eight people. The thing to do, of course, is to reserve the whole place and throw a party (about ¥8000/person). It's like eating in Grandmother's kitchen. Mrs. Hotta will arrange your menu for you, which means you'll likely have a little of whatever she has in the pot that day. You will not be disappointed. She'll also cater, supplying such American feasts as roast turkey. Reserve three or four days in advance.

2-3-8 Minami-Aoyama, Minato-ku. Hours: 6 p.m.–midnight. Closed Sun. & hol. Tel: 3404-8995.

Best Churrasco

BACANA features *churrasco,* chicken, beef, or pork grilled on spits that look a lot like swords, brought to you at your table and cut to your appetite. This is a great place for carnivores. Try the all-you-can-eat *churrasco estilo rodizo* course for ¥3000, where they will keep coming until you tell them to stop, and which includes fried potatoes, fried gyoza and buttered rice. This is clearly not health food. Or, for the same price, the mini *churrasco* and "stamina" stew. You have to choose one of the two courses. The house offers many other Brazilian specialties, like *feijoada,* black beans, meat and rice; *couve,* green vegetables cooked with garlic, and of course drinks made with *pinga,* the South American paint remover made from sugar cane. Last but not least is the frenetic music featured every night, during which conga lines of several dozen people are not uncommon. Best, only really, day to go is

Sunday, when many of the city's Brazilians show up. Other nights the clientele leans more to the salaryman/ college kid types. In the new BEAM building.

BEAM Bldg. 6F, 31-2 Udagawacho, Shibuya-ku. Hours: 11:30 a.m.–2 p.m., 5–11 p.m. (11:30 a.m.–11 p.m. on Sat., Sun., & hol.) Tel: 5489-0109. *See Shibuya map.*

Best British Food

1066, Naka-Meguro. Okay, nobody goes to England for the food. It's an old joke. But do yourself a favor and sample the fare offered here. Not just another pub filled with non-Brit dart throwers, the atmosphere is refined but not snobbish. The tasteful decor and genuine British customers add authenticity, the food is delicious (not just Japanized British pub food) and elegantly served. Squab pie, kippers, cod, etc. On Sundays there is a "Roast Lunch," featuring roast beef and roast pork. And don't forget the four kinds of English beer on tap. Good show!

3-9-5 Kami-Meguro, Meguro-ku. Hours: teatime: 4–6 p.m., dinner: 5:30–10:30 p.m. Closed Mondays unless you wish to reserve it for a suitable number of customers. Tel: 3719-9059.

GENERAL

Best Hamburger

A Big Mac is a joke and a Whopper's a wimp up against **ARI'S LAMPLIGHT**'s whopping big burger with all the trimmings. It comes in three sizes, and is best with a mug of draft. To fail to accompany this heavenly hamburger with an order of Ari's onion rings (more accurately, onion ring tempura) would be a sin. Ari's itself, a piano bar, is a bastion of crooning and warbling regulars who get endless enjoyment out of singing "Memories" one more time, and the place is especially lively, in its own way, on the last Friday of the month. The slightly seedy American decor gives the feeling that you have just walked into the bar of the Omaha Holiday Inn. It's across the street from the Fuji Film Building on Roppongi Dori.

Odakyu Minami-Aoyama Bldg. B1. 7-8-1 Minami-Aoyama, Minato-ku. Hours: 11:30 a.m.–1:45 p.m., 5:30 p.m.–2 a.m. Closed Sun & hol. Tel: 3499-1573.

Best Company Cafeteria

All big companies maintain a cafeteria to feed, extremely cheaply, their employees, and the **TOKYO CITY HALL (TOCHO)** is no exception, except that, being a public building, the public has access to it as well. The food is no better or worse than most cheap places in Shinjuku, but the prices are rock-bottom. Open from 10 a.m.–5 p.m. for coffee and light meals, Lunch is served from 11:30 a.m.–2 p.m., when there are a variety of very cheap set menus to choose from. *Ramen* is only ¥300. But show us a place where you can dine at these prices while enjoying a view like this (it's on the 32nd floor).

Best Onion Rings

TONY ROMA'S, Roppongi & Aoyama. This is more an onion ring loaf than a serving. Pick it apart with your fingers, lather it with catsup, and know heaven. TR also has great spare ribs and a decent chef's salad. (And a great outdoor location on the river at Enoshima Beach.)

5-4-20 Roppongi, Minato-ku. Hours: 5–10:30 p.m. (until 1 a.m. Fri. & Sat., 4–10:30 p.m. on Sun.). Tel: 3408-2748. *See Roppongi map.*

Sumitomo Seimei Bldg. B1. 3-1-30 Minami-Aoyama, Minato-ku. Hours: noon–2:30 p.m., 5–10:30 p.m., noon–10:30 p.m. on Sat., Sun., & hol. Tel: 3479-5214.

Best Brunches

Tops is **L'ORANGERIE**, Aoyama. Located at the top of the Hanae Mori Building on Omotesando, this elegant restaurant has everything you could want in a Sunday brunch—good breakfast fare, lots of it (it's a buffet), and in an opulent setting. Good French-roast coffee with refills, too. ¥3500. And after sating your appetite, you can join the ongoing fashion parade with a stroll down Omotesando, Tokyo's self-styled Champs Elysées.

3-6-1 Kita-Aoyama, Minato-ku. Hours: 11:30 a.m.–2:30 p.m., 5:30–9:30 p.m. daily. Sunday brunch: 11 a.m.–2:30 p.m. Tel: 3407-7461. *See Aoyama/Harajuku map.*

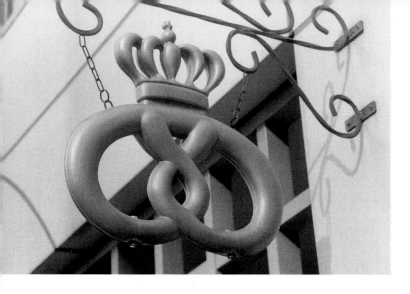

The **CAPITOL TOKYU** in Akasaka (formerly the Hilton) is also a good bet for a leisurely, "Old Tokyo" meal, but it's a breakfast buffet rather than a brunch, served in the Tea Lounge every day. On Saturdays and Sundays, it runs until noon. There are few more mellow ways to enjoy a meal for those who find themselves alone in this city than to eat breakfast while perusing a newspaper at a table overlooking the hotel's traditional Japanese garden.

2-10-3 Nagatacho, Chiyoda-ku. Hours: 7 a.m.–10:30 p.m. daily. Tel: 3581-4511. *See Akasaka map.*

Best Hip Health Food

MOMINOKI, Harajuku. This is a place where health food adherents can go for an elegant evening out, proving that health food does not necessarily have to be a Spartan pursuit. Not at all. Mominoki's multi-level atmosphere is intriguing and the clientele not your average salaryman or college-kid crowd. Meals are served on beautiful, hand-made pottery dishes. Try the cake; they have several good varieties. To top it all off, a jazz pianist plays softly in the background a few times a month. Health Heaven. Obviously not the alfalfa-sprout approach to healthy eating, Mominoki also serves meat and fish dishes, but of course cooks them in a healthy way.

2-18-5 Jingumae, Shibuya-ku. Hours: 11 a.m.–11 p.m. Closed Sun. Tel: 3405-9144. See Aoyama/Harajuku map.

Best Health Food

TENMI, Shibuya. This mellow place used to be a favorite of John Lennon's, and it is still a daily stop for some of the more health-minded folk in Tokyo. And the reason is easy to see: they make health food taste good. The vegetarian goodies that accompany the ¥1030 *genmai* (brown rice) *teishoku* (lunch set) complement it well. Soothing Japanese-style interior and a health food grocery on the ground floor, where you can buy things like vitamins and natural potato chips, are an added bonus.

Daiichi Iwashita Bldg. 2F. 1-10-6 Jinnan, Shibuya-ku. Hours: 11:30 a.m.–1:55 p.m., 5:30–8:50 p.m. Closed 2nd & 3rd Wed. Tel: 3496-9703. See Shibuya map.

Best Garlic Restaurant

NINNIKUYA, Ebisu. It means "house of garlic," and you can smell it a block away. Not a classifiable restaurant in terms of nationality or type of food, Ninnikuya just serves anything cooked anywhere in the world—as long as it is cooked with garlic. Thai garlic chicken, garlic rice, garlic bread, and so on. Hearty, happy crowds at all times, and worth any wait you may encounter. Go on a week-night to minimize the crowds (preferably on the eve of a day when you have no plans to go near anyone you are not dining with that night). The restaurant is a bit hard to find, so we suggest you call for directions, and get there early, because it's always crowded.

1-26-12 Ebisu, Shibuya-ku. Hours: 6:15 p.m.–10:30 p.m. Closed Sun. & hol. Tel: 3446-5887.

Best Eclectic Restaurants

KURI-KURI. If you had to classify this place, you'd have to call it African. The owners are well traveled and have brought the world's tastes back with them. Comfortable place with antiques and menus in children's books. Try the sangria. Take the Odakyu Line to Sangubashi Station. Exit the station and follow the freeway (20 min. on foot) until you see the sign for Kuri-Kuri.

3-38-12 Yoyogi, Shibuya-ku. Hours: 5 p.m.–midnight. Closed Tues. & hol. Tel: 5388-9376.

And no place is more unclassifiable than **ICHIOKU**, the funky little place in Roppongi. Cheese *gyoza*, oysters, mushrooms in sauce, great salads, and a tofu steak for only ¥250. The menu is in pictures under the glass table tops, and you write your own order. The atmosphere is as eclectic as the food, and Ueda-san, the owner and creator of these unusual, savory dishes, is also in a class by himself. Now serving some delicious ¥1000 lunches.

4-4-5 Roppongi, Minato-ku. Hours: 11:30 a.m.–1:30 p.m. (weekdays), 5 p.m.–midnight. (6–11 p.m. on Sun.) Tel: 3405-9891. *See Roppongi map.*

Best Bagels

FOX BAGELS, Roppongi. Lyle Fox is something of a legend when bakers of Japan get together and talk about baking's greats. No, seriously, he introduced this delicious Jewish-American bread to Japan in 1981 and has since been featured in just about every magazine and on every TV channel in the country. More amazing still, some have taken to referring to TV Asahi Dori, so named for the channel 10 broadcast center at the top of the

street, as "Bagel Dori." Whatever. Fox remains, despite some attempts at imitation, the best bagel man in town. At his shop on Bagel Dori he makes bagel sandwiches to eat there or take out, and offers sausages, bagel dogs, New York-style cheesecake, and some great brownies. Also a variety of deli sandwiches.

6-15-19 Roppongi, Minato-ku. Hours: 8 a.m.–8 p.m. daily. Tel: 3403-7638. *See Roppongi map.*

Best Late-Night Dining

Tokyo's premier restauranteur, Kozo Hasegawa, has for years been using his unique talent for knowing what the dining and drinking public wants to open a series of restaurants in Tokyo. The food is always good, the atmosphere comfortable, even daring at some places, and all but the Harajuku Zest Annex are open until 5 a.m. You can't go wrong with **LA BOHEME** or **ZEST**.

Harajuku La Boheme: Jingubashi Bldg. 2F, 6-7-18 Jingumae, Shibuya-ku. Tel: 3400-3406.

Kasumicho La Boheme: Azabu Palace 2F, 2-25-18 Nishi Azabu, Minato-ku. Tel: 3407-1363.

Daikanyama La Boheme: Kinjoryokosha Bldg. 1F, B1, 16-2 Daikanyamacho, Shibuya-ku. Tel: 3476-4799.

Minami-Aoyama La Boheme: Kaneko Bldg. 1F, 7-11-4 Minami-Aoyama, Minato-ku. Tel: 3499-3377.

Setagaya La Boheme. Maison de Soleil 1F, B1, 1 9 11 Ikejiri, Setagaya-ku. Tel: 5486-1021/2.

Shibuya La Boheme: Campari Bldg. 13F, 1-6-8 Jinnan, Shibuya-ku. Tel: 3477-0481.

Roppongi La Boheme: 1F Lundic Bldg., 4-11-13 Roppongi, Minato-ku. Tel: 3478-0222.

* * *

Harajuku Zest: B1 Jingumae Bldg., 6-7-18 Jingumae, Shibuya-ku. Tel: 3409-6268.

Harajuku Zest Annex: B1 Iida Bldg., 5-8-7 Jingumae, Shibuya-ku. Hours: 5 p.m.–5 a.m. Tel: 3499-0293.

Setagaya Zest: 3-29-4 Ikejiri, Setagaya-ku. Tel: 5486-0321/2

Nishi Azabu Zest: 2F Yokoshiba Daini Bldg., 2-13-15 Nishi Azabu, Minato-ku. Tel: 3400-2235.

Best Salad Bar

VICTORIA STATION, Roppongi, Akasaka, Shibuya, Shinjuku. It's well known that Victoria Station is a good place for prime rib or a steak, but vegetarians should know about the salad bars. There are about 20 items to choose from, and toppings like sunflower seeds, and, of course, croutons. It comes with most entrees, but you can order salad alone and go back as many times as you like.

Shibuya: Chitose Kaikan 2F. 13 Udagawacho, Shibuya-ku. Hours: 11 a.m.–1 a.m. daily. Tel: 3463-5288. *See Shibuya map.*

Roppongi: 4-9-2 Roppongi, Minato-ku. Hours: 11 a.m.–11 p.m. daily. Tel: 3479-4601. *See Roppongi map.*

Akasaka: 3-15-13 Akasaka, Minato-ku. Hours: 11 a.m.–11 p.m. daily. Tel: 3586-0711. *See Akasaka map.*

Shinjuku: 3-16-5 Toyama, Shinjuku-ku. Hours: 11 a.m.–3 a.m. Tel: 3205-0844.

Best Pizza

Sure you can get pizza in 30 minutes or less from Domino's, Pizza Station, Manhattan Pizza and new-guy-on-the-scooter, Pizza Hut, but we aren't going to put on weight trying them all out. So winner of the non-delivered pizza award goes to **IL FORNO**, in Roppongi's Piramide Building. It's not an Italian place as such, rather a clone of a Santa Monica, California bistro, but then pizza ain't really Italian either, is it? It's a bright and airy place, with a health-conscious menu and reasonable prices.

6-6-9 Roppongi, Minato-ku. Hours: 11 a.m.–11 p.m. daily. Tel: 3796-2642. *See Roppongi map.*

Drinking

飲
物

Best Drinking Neighborhood

GOLDEN GAI, Shinjuku. There is no shortage of places to imbibe your favorite booze in this city, but our vote for the best bar experience goes to this warren of tiny, specialized drinkeries. John Kennerdell, who knows what he's talking about, supplied us with this view of the neighborhood . . . .

The year was 1949 and MacArthur's GHQ had had its fill of the food and drink stalls clogging the streets in front of Shinjuku Station. Clear out, said the authorities, and suggested an alternative location: a corner of Kabukicho waist-high in weeds, still province of badgers and foxes, and (women were warned), randy highwaymen. So was born Golden Gai, the last in a grand tradition of minia-ture, maze-like entertainment districts. Some 240 shops and perhaps 400 people share this quarter of a city block; despite its seedy looks and dubious reputation, it is, essentially, a village. Its reputation, historically anyhow, includes tales of *boryoku baa,* ("violence bars," i.e. *yakuza* haunts), drug dealings, and prostitution. Traces of the latter can be seen in the way the buildings are constructed: bar on the ground floor, steep staircase to the owner's quarters on the second, even steeper ladder to a pair of one-and-a-half-mat "customer" rooms on the third floor. These days, a number of the second floors have become bars in their own right, but the owners still live on the premises. It's not an easy place for recommendations. These bars exist for their regulars, many of whom have been coming for decades. Roughly a quarter of the shops are figured to be clip joints, the sure sign of which is an invitation from a man in drag. These caveats aside, Golden Gai offers the kind of casual, authentic friendli-ness that modern, urban Japan tends to forget. Try the bigger, "public" bars like Von's and Hungry Humphrey (both on the corner opposite the police box). Friends made here can often introduce you to the smaller, more private places. Or simply stroll these alleys—you'll eventually meet people anyway, and see a great deal besides. But do it soon. Golden Gai has already survived a year or two longer than anyone really expected it would. Further miracles, in our brave new world of Tokyo land prices, seem unlikely. To find Golden Gai, ask directions to Hanazono Shrine, which is near the intersection of Meiji Dori and Yasukuni Dori. Golden Gai is located right behind it. See Shinjuku map.

Best Beer Hall

LION, Ginza. High ceilings, confused architecture, and better than average beer-hall food make this old standard a good place to grab a brew and a bite. A Ginza tradition since 1934.

7-9-20 Ginza, Chuo-ku. Hours: 11:30 a.m.–11 p.m. daily. Tel: 3571-2590. *See Ginza map.*

Best German Beer Hall

BEI RUDI is unusual in a variety of ways, not least in that is has remained unchanged for years. They serve up, in addition to a wonderful variety of beers, including Lowenbrau on tap, some great cholesterol-intensive dishes like pigs' knuckles. Also novel here is the German band and singing that goes on every night. Festive.

1-11-45 Akasaka, Minato-ku. Hours: 5 p.m.–midnight. Closed Sun. & hol. Tel: 3583-2519.

Best Beer Garden

HANEZAWA GARDENS, Hiro-o. Wanting a cold one outdoors on a hot summer day? Try this pleasant beer garden in the middle of a quiet residential district. Since the sun goes down at about 7 p.m. during the summer, an early evening spent here has a way of changing character as the light dims and the beer flows. Usual Japanese beer-garden snacks also available.

3-12-15 Hiro-o, Shibuya-ku. Hours: 5–8:30 p.m. from April 1 until it gets too cold to eat outside. Tel: 3400-2013.

Best Latin Hangouts

BODEGUITA, Ebisu. This "salsa/Cuban spot" sways sensuously each night to recorded Latin rhythms enhanced sometimes by customers beating away on the various percussion instruments strewn about. It's crowded and has just a hint of seediness, the kind of atmosphere that's hard to find in form-over-function Tokyo. Open until midnight most nights, later on Fridays and Saturdays. Behind the Dai-ichi Kangyo Bank ("heart" bank) to the left of the main entrance of Ebisu Station.

New Life Ebisu Bldg. 2F. 1-7-3 Ebisu Minami, Shibuya-ku. Hours: 6 p.m.–midnight, later on weekends if the crowd warrants. Closed Sun. & hol. Tel: 3715-7721.

ACARAJÉ in Nishi Azabu has long been a popular spot with Brazilians and other South American people, but to try to categorize this crowd would be a mistake. English, French, Americans, Italians and many others who include Acarajé on their regular pub crawls mingle happily. We even met a couple of Bulgarians there. It's unpretentious and fun, mainly because of the infectious friendliness of Andy (pronounced "Angie"), the owner. A pretty good selection of Brazilian dishes, lively latin music and some *pinga*-based cocktails, like *caipirinhas*, that will take the enamel off your teeth. *Saude*.

1-8-19 Nishi-Azabu, Minato-ku (behind Sunset Strip). Hours: 6 p.m.(maybe)–whenever. Closed Mon. Tel: 3401-0973. See Roppongi map.

Best Saké Sampling

The Japanese make 6000 different kinds of saké, and **NIHONSHU CENTER** is the place to visit if you want to know where any or all of these are made and where they are available. Meanwhile, for ¥300, you can sample five suggested brews (cold in summer, hot in winter), and keep the cup. Saké brewing and its history are explained, and there's a reference library on the second floor.

5-9-1 Ginza, Chuo-ku. Hours: 10:30 a.m. – 6:30 p.m. Closed Thurs., 4th Sun. & hol. Tel: 3575-0656. See Ginza map.

Best Saké Pub

CHICHIBU NISHIKI, Ginza, is the perfect place to drink saké. You are in a wonderfully preserved wooden town house, surrounded by *shoji*, tatami, and antiques, all under a decidedly un-claustrophobic high ceiling. The place is the Tokyo outlet (for over 60 years) of the saké manufacturer of the same name over in neighboring Saitama Prefecture, who is obviously not driven by any incentive to make a profit, as a *tokkuri* of the house brew starts at only ¥600. Drinking is the main attraction here, but the dishes offered to enhance this pleasant experience need not take a back seat.

2-13-14 Ginza, Chuo-ku. Hours: 5–10:30 p.m. Closed Sun. & hol. Tel: 3541-4777. See Ginza map.

Best Brew with a View

A few years ago, to the distress of many Edokko, Asahi Beer razed their classic beer hall across the bridge from Asakusa subway station and built in its place an ugly stone monolith topped with a great gold glob that has been described as resembling a variety of things, from a "frozen flame" to less complimentary descriptions, usually involving bodily fluids. Time marches on. But the building next to this, with the gold windows and faceted white top, Asahi's corporate headquarters, has on the 22nd floor a little beer hall called **SKYROOM**, that commands a

wonderful view of this historical area. Beer is only ¥500, and most of the seats face the windows. It's rarely crowded, and a great place to set a spell to relax and get away from the bustle of Asakusa.

1-23-1 Azumabashi, Sumida-ku. Hours: 10 a.m.–8:30 p.m. Tel: 5608-5357.

Best Roppongi Bar

Well, Roppongi being what it is, some people would be surprised to know that there is even a good one. They're all perceived as having dirty toilets and being full of cigarette smoke and rude drunks. But there is indeed a spot where you can sip a beer, be largely free of cigarette smoke, and enjoy continuous entertainment all for just the price of a beer. It's the "Mister Donut" corner, where, just in front of the Roi Building, there's a low planter to sit on. Just elbow your way through the yuppies at Le Mistral Bleu (called the "train bar") to get a can of beer, go outside, and find a spot. The parade of Roppongi lookers, hookers, hawkers, and gawkers never ends, not even as it's getting light on a fuzzy summer morn. Urban hanging out at its best. No phone.

Best After-hours, Third World Hangout

PIP'S in Roppongi, across from Mister Donut. This dive has somehow become the after-work refuge of choice for hundreds of Tokyo's many Asian working girls and boys. A good time to go is Saturday night after one or two in the

morning. The atmosphere is thick with street-smartness, the social tone wary and a bit insular. After all, these people just got off work and no longer have to be particularly charming to you or to anyone else. They just want to have a drink and talk over the evening with their friends. A sprinkling of posing military types adds just the right touch of seediness to make this a great stop for a last drink.

Shuwa Bldg. B1. 3-4-12 Roppongi, Minato-ku, Hours: 5 p.m.– 5 a.m. daily. Tel: 3470-0857. *See Roppongi map.*

Best American Bar/Restaurant

HARD ROCK CAFÉ, Roppongi. Tokyo's homage to the gods of rock 'n' roll, this reliable watering hole, like its counterparts in other major world cities, offers good drinks, simple American fare (club sandwiches, hamburgers, salads), and a parade of interesting customers. Deco-rated, like all good Hard Rock Cafés, with gold records and guitars autographed by their famous players. The background music constantly strives to be more than background music, making your "Come here often?" a bit hard to get across, but, hey, remember that this is the Hard Rock.

5-4-20 Roppongi, Minato-ku. Hours: 11:30 a.m.–2 a.m. daily; until 4 a.m. on Fri. & Sat. and 11:30 p.m. on Sun. Tel: 3408-7018. *See Roppongi map.*

Shopping

買物

GENERAL SHOPS

Best Total Shopping Experience

PARCO, Shibuya. This is a toughie, but Parco (Parts 1,2,3, & "Quattro") seems to have the art of shopping covered just a bit better than its many worthy competitors. Each of the four Parco buildings has its own character. Part 1 specializes in non-designer things, as well as shoes, bags, jewelry, and make-up. Aimed at the younger set, the place is set up to provide the shopper with every reason to stay in the store during breaks in the buying. A well-balanced selection of good restaurants offer Italian, Japanese, Russian, and a few other types of cuisine. Then there's a theater, an art gallery, gift shops, and a bookstore. Part 2 is for designer boutiques, Part 3 for home, office, and personal accessories, and Quattro for imported designer brands for men. Quattro sports a live-music club also called Quattro, a hip place that has the flexibility to accommodate a variety of events from supper-club shows to dancing or theater presentations.

15-1 Udagawacho, Shibuya-ku. Hours: 10 a.m.–8:30 p.m. Quattro Bldg. until 9 p.m. (Restaurants: 11 a.m.–10 p.m.). Tel: 3464-5111. See Shibuya map.

Best Designer Anything

AXIS, Roppongi. The key word in this complex is "design." Even the building itself is an example of gray-and-black Tokyo post-modern design. Within are 20 independent shops selling furniture, household, kitchen, and office things into which someone has put a lot of thought, at least on how to make them look better, and sometimes even work better. Mostly imported items, but some very tasteful Japanese bursts of creativity can be found as well. Totally free of such tiresome things as bargains, a stroll through the AXIS building is always fun.

5-17-1 Roppongi, Minato-ku. Hours: 11 a.m.–7 p.m. Closed Sun. & hol. Tel: 3587-2781. See Roppongi map.

Best Toy Shops

For little kids: **SANRIO GALLERY**, Ginza. This is truly a bit of Wonderland. Sanrio has already demonstrated its marketing acumen with a worldwide network of outlets for the "Hello Kitty" line and others, so what's one more store? Statement perhaps, but what a fun statement. You enter via an escalator that escalates through an enchanted forest, and from beginning to end your steps are guided— slowly, so you don't hurry past a miracle or two. Try to catch the expressions of the toddlers when the tree near the escalator begins to talk. How about a miniature, gas-powered Ferrari Testerosa for a price just shy of a real Nissan 300ZX without the radio? It's all here.

Iwasaki Bldg. 2-7-17 Ginza, Chuo-ku. Hours: 11 a.m.–8 p.m. Closed 1st, 3rd, & 4th Tues. Tel: 3563-2731. See Ginza map.

Most lively: **KIDDYLAND**, Harajuku. Everyone knows what fun Japanese toy stores are. You can play with the toys before you decide to buy one of your own to wreck. Kiddyland has seven floors of tooting, smiling, squawking, musical, realistic things to play with. Computer games, practical jokes, masks, things that throw, things to throw on someone else, things that fly, roll, waddle, and

tumble. The place is madness any day of the week, utter madness on weekends.

6-1-9 Jingumae, Shibuya-ku. Hours: 10 a.m.–8 p.m. Closed 3rd Tues., Tel: 3409-3431. *See Aoyama/Harajuku map.*

Biggest: **HAKUHINKAN TOY PARK**, Ginza. Somewhat less frantic than Kiddyland, this place has an equally broad selection of things to play with. Exceptional doll department on the 4th floor.

8-8-11 Ginza, Chuo-ku. Hours: 11 a.m.–8 p.m. daily. Tel: 3571-8008. *See Ginza map.*

Best Russian Stuff

SHIRAKABA, Shimbashi. Some of the best things to come out of what used to be the USSR to these islands are here for the purchasing. The ceramics, dolls, toys, albums of Russian music, lacquer-ware, clothing, and such may have you thinking you've wandered into a World Fair exhibit, but there's no denying the good value of some of the many kinds of caviar, vodka (plain or flavored), lemon, juniper berry, chili pepper), and equally good beverages and delicacies from other Eastern European countries.

Ekimae Bldg. 5F, Ichigo-kan, 2-20 Shimbashi. Hours: 9 a.m.– 6 p.m.. Closed Sun. & hol. Tel: 3567-6361.

Best Model Trains

TENSHODO, Ginza. "We don't stop playing with toys," a sage once said. "The toys just get more expensive." Tenshodo offers a range of toys for the serious player. Model trains are the specialty; the store offers them in a variety of gauges and with all the extras as well as books on layouts and landscaping. The store also has a selection of gas-powered, radio-controlled cars and boats. Nifty.

4-3-9 Ginza, Chuo-ku. Hours: 10:30 a.m.–7 p.m. Closed Thurs. Tel: 3562-0021. *See Ginza map.*

Best Inedible Food

KAPPABASHI. Dealing with plastic-food menus in Tokyo is perhaps one story that all tourists take home to tell. But why not take home a bit of the plastic fantastic as well? Kappabashi wholesale market is the place to find it. (Restaurant owners put these realistic plastic sculptures on view to announce their offerings—and incidentally to receive orders from non-speakers of Japanese in sign language. Ironically enough, this practice started when Western food was being introduced in Japan to ease the doubts of Japanese diners reluctant to try it.) We suggest you take home the beer mug, complete with condensation, or the ever-popular spaghetti with a fork held up by several strands of pasta. Best thing we saw last time there was a bubbling pot of stew set atop glowing coals—giving out not the merest trace of heat. The flickering glow was a light trick and the bubbling supplied by a small air pump and hose beneath. Get there by taking the Ginza Line to Tawaramachi and head for the building with the huge chef's head on the top.

Best Wholesale Kitchen Supplies

KAPPABASHI is more than plastic food, though. Like Akihabara for electronics and Kanda for books, this area specializes in restaurant supplies. Everything that thriving industry could ever use is for sale here—industrial-strength stoves and ovens, grills, food preparation machines, silver and glassware, light fixtures, tables, chairs, stools, signs, bar rails, shakers, dispensers—and things like chopsticks and plastic cups in bulk. You can also get a real sushi chef's apron or one of those great wooden rice containers at rock-bottom prices.

Best Paper, Stationery, Party, and Wrapping Supplies

The Asakusabashi area is known for its Japanese dolls for Boys' and Girls' days, and also for its wholesalers of seasonal decorations and gift wrapping supplies. In the months preceding the New Year's, Christmas and even Halloween holidays, you can find a wide range of decora-

71

tions at almost half the price they are asking for the same things at the department stores. Among the many stores, **SHIMOJIMA** is about the biggest, operating eight stores in the area, each with six or so floors. Exit JR Sobu Line's Asakusabashi Station from the front of the train coming from Akihabara, and turn to the left and walk for about two minutes. There you'll find the store called Gift Wrap-kan, for wrapping paper, Japanese *washi*, letter sets, seasonal greeting cards, gift bags, ribbons, and boxes. Another two minutes in the same direction brings you to the store called 5-goukan, for seasonal decorations, stationery, and party goods and favors.

1-30-10 Asakusabashi, Taito-ku. Hours differ from store to store, but most are open between 9 a.m. and 5:30 p.m. Tel: 3863-5501.

Best Western-Style Supermarket

NATIONAL AZABU, Hiro-o. Centered in Tokyo's *gaijin* ghetto, which got that way because Japan's first Western envoy in centuries, Townsend Harris, took up residence in Azabu and there went the neighborhood. National Azabu exemplifies the imported-goods store. At the same time, it confirms the Westerner's fear of (and willingness to pay) the high price(s) of staying alive in Japan while altering not one bit his/her hometown eating habits. It's all here for those with the budgets, although it's hard getting used to seeing Shredded Wheat as an imported gourmet item. Great selection of cheeses, fresh herbs, range chickens, paté, and champagne.

4-5-2 Minami-Azabu, Minato-ku. Hours: 9:30 a.m.–6:30 p.m., until 7 on Sat. & Sun. Tel: 3442-3181. *See Roppongi map.*

Best English-Language Bookstores

Let's be honest. It's difficult to name the best English-language bookstore in Tokyo. A number of centrally located stores carry numerous English-language books, but the one you choose will likely depend on where you are when you decide you need a new book or have the time to browse.

East Side: **JENA**, Ginza. Head right up the escalators to the third floor, which is entirely given over to books for those who do not read any of the three forms of written Japanese. Paperbacks, classics, lots of magazines, most world newspapers, art books, picture books, reference books—mostly in English, but Jena has sizable sections for French, German, and some other languages. Bookstore browsing is cool in Japan, almost a national sport.

The Japanese can read *entire novels* while standing up at bookstores, then put the book back and go home. So spend a few hours.

5-6-1 Ginza, Chuo-ku. Hours: 10:30 a.m.–7:50 p.m., noon–6:30 p.m. on Sun. Closed hol. Tel: 3571-2980. See Ginza map.

Even bigger but less central on the east side is **MARUZEN** in Nihombashi. This comprehensive hardback bookstore first started selling books in languages other than Japanese in 1869 as part of Meiji Restoration efforts to spread all the new "outsider" knowledge.

2-3-10 Nihombashi, Chuo-ku. Hours: 10 a.m.–7 p.m. Closed Sun. Tel: 3272-7211.

West side: **KINOKUNIYA**, Shinjuku. This store is more conveniently located for many people, in the middle of Shinjuku near Isetan. The sixth floor is home to 100,000 foreign-language publications. With branches in many U.S. cities and a London office, Kinokuniya qualifies as Japan's most far-flung bookstore.

3-17-7 Shinjuku, Shinjuku-ku. Hours: 10 a.m.–7 p.m. Closed 3rd Wed. Tel: 3354-0131. See Shinjuku map.

Best Used Books

The **KANDA** district, site of many universities and other institutions of higher learning, is the book capital of this capital. Bookstores of every description can be found for about 300 meters on either side of Jimbocho Station, along the south side of Yasukuni-Dori. **KITAZAWA SHOTEN** is probably the leader, with an extensive selection of new hardback books on the first floor and an awesome collection of used volumes on the second. Browse the locked case of first editions. A few of the other stores are **MATSUMURA SHOTEN** for art books, and **KANDA KOSHO CENTER**, where in 11 shops you can find old movie posters, maps, old prints, magazines, and comic books. Hundreds of other bookstores are in this area, and with its Left Bank atmosphere (Tokyo style), it's a pleasant place for a stroll as well.

Kitazawa Shoten: 2-5 Jimbocho, Kanda, Chiyoda-ku. Hours: 10 a.m.–6 p.m. Closed Sun. & hol. Tel: 3263-0011.

Matsumura Shoten: 1-7-5 Jimbocho, Kanda, Chiyoda-ku. Hours: 10:30 a.m.–6 p.m. Closed Sun. & hol. Tel: 3291-2410 or 3295-5678.

Kanda Kosho Center: 2-3 Jimbocho, Kanda, Chiyoda-ku.

Hours vary with each shop, but most stay open until around 6:30 p.m. Closed Sun. & hol.

Best Japanese-Language Textbooks

BONJINSHA. The place for anyone wanting to learn or teach the Japanese language. In addition to textbooks, you'll find almost 2000 dictionaries, cassette tapes, and videos.

Kojimachi New Yahiko Bldg. 2F. 6-2 Kojimachi, Chiyoda-ku. Hours: 10 a.m.–7 p.m. Closed Sun. & hol. Tel: 3239-8673.

Best Bibles

KYOBUNKAN has to be the most complete collection of books on religion in a Buddhist country. Bibles in Greek,

Hindi, Hebrew, and even Arabic. Volumes on all religions from Ainu creeds to Zoroastrian philosophy. The entrance to this store is around the side of the building that houses the regular bookstore of the same name.

Kyobunkan 3F, 4-5-1 Ginza, Chuo-ku. Hours: 10 a.m.–7 p.m. (1–5 p.m. on Sun.). Tel: 3561-8446. *See Ginza map.*

Best Postcards

ON SUNDAYS, Aoyama on Killer-Dori. This place should be in Berkeley. Quiet and definitely cool, On Sundays offers the biggest collection we've seen of art postcards. Old movie stars and scenes, works by classic photographers, designs new and old. Refreshingly understated when compared to the Hallmark-hall-of-cleverness atmosphere at greeting-card sections in other stores. Also art books you may find nowhere else and some posters. The Galerie Watari next door has shown such artists as Andy Warhol, Keith Haring, and Buckminster Fuller (yes, artist). Note: since this writing, the funky old location has been razed and the postcards, etc., are now next door in a decidedly more sanitized atmosphere. The merchandise is still the best, so it stays in the book, but why oh why does this city eat its soul so?

3-7-6 Jingumae, Shibuya-ku. Hours: 11 a.m.–9 p.m. Closed Mon. Tel: 3470-1424. *See Aoyama/Harajuku map.*

Best Office Supplies

ITO-YA, Ginza. What Tokyu Hands is to the home, Ito-ya is to the office. A must for office-supply-store addicts. You know who you are. Breaking away from the greeting-card selection on the ground floor, you encounter the mezzanine-level section devoted to personal calendars and quality pens. The other seven floors offer complete selections of artists' tools and materials, stationery supplies, Japanese paper, hobby supplies, drafting gear and tables, furniture, and so on. Even if you don't want to buy anything, this place is a fun browse. There is a printing service at their graphic designer's heaven, known as Ito-ya 2, behind the Ginza main store.

2-7-15 Ginza, Chuo-ku. Hours: 9:30 a.m.–7 p.m., 10 a.m.– 6 p.m. on Sun. & hol. Tel: 3561-8311. *See Ginza map.*

Best Art Books

LOGOS, Parco Part 1, Shibuya. Need a new copy of *Mr. Scott's Guide to the Enterprise?* The basement floor of Parco (that's the one with the giant airplane wing at the entrance) houses, among other things, this and hundreds of other art and hobby books. You'll find large-format books on art, movies, theater, architecture, design, photography, and hobbies. Maps, magazines, guidebooks, and posters, too.

Parco Part 1, BF. 15-1 Udagawacho, Shibuya-ku. Hours: 10 a.m.–8:30 p.m. daily. Tel: 3496-7362. See Shibuya map.

Best Record Shop

WAVE, Roppongi. You want to find a certain tune, a certain symphony or play. WAVE probably has it in seven different versions. The Seibu Saison Group shows how state-of-the-art application of Japanese marketing can turn a record store into a shopping experience. (They did the "concept" stores SEED and LOFT in Shibuya as well.) WAVE is a fun place to spend too much money for recorded music. The first floor offers new releases on LP, CD, and video. The innovative displays/promotions in the massive front window change monthly. The second floor is for pop tapes, video sales, and audio/video accessories. Three features pop CDs, ethnic and miscellaneous CDs and LPs. Four is for jazz and classical CDs, and little musical and percussion things you can play. There's a movie theater in the basement, Cine Saison, that shows foreign and art films. Art Vivant bookstore on the fourth floor is a great source for hip magazines, as well as deluxe and underground art/photography books.

6-2-27 Roppongi, Minato-ku. Hours: 11 a.m.–9 p.m. (until 8 p.m. on Sun.). Closed 1st and 3rd Wed. Tel: 3408-0111. *See Roppongi map.*

Perhaps Roppongi is a bit out of the way for you. **HMV** in Shinjuku and Harajuku, and **VIRGIN MEGASTORE** in Shibuya, both built since WAVE opened, come very close indeed to matching that store's comprehensive stock. Indeed, WAVE has recently had to completely redesign its facilities to keep up with these two energetic record merchandisers.

HMV: 28-6 Udagawacho, Shibuya-ku. Hours: 10 a.m.–10 p.m. (1st floor until 9 p.m.) daily. Tel: 3477-6880.

HMV: B1 Laforet Bldg., 1-11-6 Jingumae, Shibuya-ku. Hours: 11 a.m.–8 p.m. daily. Tel: 3423-4891.

Virgin Megastore: B1 Marui Shinjuku. Hours: 10:30 a.m.–8 p.m. Closed Wed. Tel: 3353-0038.

Best Radio Programs in Your Own Language

A **SHORTWAVE RADIO** is one way many foreigners have discovered to keep in touch with home, wherever that is. The selection of bilingual TV movies is far from the best, and they are mostly in English. Bilingual TV news concentrates overmuch on local events and politics, and the Far East Network (FEN) only offers five minutes of news an hour and a few news programs. But with recent advances in electronic circuitry, even a modest shortwave radio will outperform that coveted, old-time Zenith Transoceanic that we usually associate with shortwave communications. So if you know what time to tune in, and guides are available, you can listen to the unbiased (or at least alternatively biased) news from home. Spend at least ¥40,000 and be sure it has digital tuning and a scanner. And to not include the Sony AN-1 outdoor antenna, with its powered signal-booster, is to have thrown all that money away. Have fun. **X-ONE**, in Akihabara, is by far Tokyo's best-stocked shop for this kind of thing. From the railway bridge in central Akihabara, look north a block or so. The vertical X-One sign is on the left.

X-One: 3-13-7 Soto Kanda, Chiyoda-ku. Hours: 10 a.m.–6:30 p.m. Closed 2nd & 4th Wed. Tel: 3255-5461.

Best Music Shop

YAMAHA SHOWROOM, Ginza. Philharmonic orchestras have to shop somewhere, and this is where they go. In addition to the extensive record and CD shop on the ground floor sharing space with a few displays of Yamaha stereo equipment, there are two floors above containing everything and then some that a 150-piece orchestra could possibly need to make sound. One of the city's best collections of classical sheet music and music books is to be found in the basement, and Yamaha Hall, on the 4th floor, is a venue for small concerts and films.

7-9-14 Ginza, Chuo-ku. Hours: 10:30 a.m.–7 p.m., until 6:30 p.m. on Sun. & hol. Closed 3rd Tues. Tel: 3572-3133. *See Ginza map.*

Best Music Boxes

NOF ANTIQUES SHELLMAN INC., Akasaka. This is a truly awe-inspiring shop. History is here. For NOF Antiques Shellman deals in music boxes, and the sky's the limit. Consider that the music box was the prototype home entertainment system. And if you're thinking of "Twinkle Twinkle Little Star" being plucked by a watch movement, maybe you'd better visit this place. One bureau-sized Swiss machine, over 150 years old, plays a perforated 20-inch steel disk through such an effective series of baffles as to give it the sound of a whole orchestra. A grand player piano asks you not to touch, please, unless of course you've got the ¥50 million they want to take it home.

2-2-19 Akasaka, Minato-ku. Hours: 10 a.m.–7 p.m., until 3 p.m. on Sat. Closed Sun. & hol. Tel: 3584-1181. *See Akasaka map.*

Best 365-Days-a-Year Discount Electronics Carnival

AKIHABARA. With people buying Japanese cameras in the States for less than they cost here, news of a section of town devoted to the Great Electron may not be earth-shaking. But this is entertainment. You owe it to yourself to wander through the labyrinth we call Akihabara. Speakers, amps, video players, cameras, and TVs stand next to refrigerators, air conditioners, fans, and kitchen appliances—all of them in a fantastic range of sizes, colors, and sounds. And all turned on. Accessible on three JR lines (the Yamanote, Keihin Tohoku, and the Sobu), as well as the Hibiya subway line (the Ginza Line's Suehirocho Station and the Toei Shinjuku Line's Iwamotocho Station are also nearby), the place is easy to reach. The thing to do is head for the big, flashy places like **YAMAGIWA** to learn what is available, and to decide what to buy, then to dive into the matrix of small shops, model number in hand, to get the best price. A little bargaining is possible, but these guys have already shaved off as much from the list price as they can and still pay the rent. Sell your equipment or pick up some bargains at **DYNAMIC AUDIO**.

Yamagiwa (main store): 4-1-1 Soto Kanda, Chiyoda-ku. Hours: 10 a.m.–7:30 p.m. Closed 2nd Wed. Tel: 3253-2111.

Dynamic Audio (trade center): 1-2-5 Soto Kanda, Chiyoda-ku. Hours: 10 a.m.–7 p.m. Closed Thurs. Tel: 3253-2001.

Best Modern Japanese Fabrics

NUNO is where renowned fabric designer Jun'ichi Arai (who often provides fabrics for Issey Miyake) offers his work for your inspection and purchase. It's such a pleasant place that you suddenly find it hard to resist picking up a pillow, or a piece of clothing or, if you sew, some of his tasteful yardage to play with on your own. The low, modern table at the center of the room adds a workroom air of casual creativity to the already congenial atmosphere, and the friendly staff will sew up a pillow or skirt in the fabric of your choice if you wish. It's in the basement of Roppongi's AXIS Building, with a branch in Matsuya Department Store in Ginza.

Roppongi AXIS Bldg. B1. 5-17-1 Roppongi, Minato-ku. Hours: 11 a.m.–7 p.m. (until 6:30 p.m. on hol.) Closed Sun. Tel: 3582-7997. *See Roppongi map.*

Best-lit Store

LIVINA YAMAGIWA, Akihabara. This is the "designer lighting" arm of the mighty Yamagiwa electronics marketing organization. Off the main street but easily found (it shines), the seven floors of this place offer you several thousand ways to bring light to dark places. They range from the subdued to the totally garish (the chandelier floor is especially tinkly), from the designer-designed to the unrelentingly functional. The prize for window shoppers is the top floor where they sell all the whirling, flashing, multi-colored, strobed, in-the-floor, smoking, screaming, and bubbling things you usually see fastened (securely, we hope) to the ceilings of dark, drunken discos.

1-5 10 Soto Kanda, Chiyoda-ku. Hours: 10 a.m.–7 p.m. Tel: 3253-2111.

Best Shoe Shop

WASHINGTON, in Ginza, could be more accurately called a department store for shoes. Seven floors of things to put on your feet, both domestic and imported—big shoes, order-made shoes, designer shoes. The place is ideal for shoppers who could be described as Imeldic. Repairs are also done. On Chuo Dori, Ginza's main street.

5-7-7 Ginza, Chuo-ku. Hours: 10:30 a.m.–8 p.m. daily. Tel: 3572-5911. *See Ginza map.*

Best Decidedly Inelegant Party Supplies

WHOOPEE, Nishi-Azabu. Naughty novelties. Every city has one of these shops, and this is Tokyo's. Stop by on your way to the party that asked you to bring a "joke gift." This place is piled high with the jokes. Every novelty you've ever heard of and quite a few you've probably never imagined. Go on in and poke around and giggle for a while. They're used to it.

2-25-19 Nishi-Azabu, Minato-ku. Hours: noon–4 a.m. daily. Tel: 3400-1963. *See Roppongi map.*

Best Buttons and Bows

OKADAYA, Shinjuku. And everything else you could possibly need for sewing. A total of 10 floors (in three locations) filled with buttons, bows, fabrics, accessories, patterns, and lots, lots more.

3-23-17 Shinjuku, Shinjuku-ku. Hours: 10 a.m.–8:30 p.m. Tel: 3352-5411. *See Shinjuku map.*

Best Travel Supplies

TCAT. It will not be the fault of Tokyo City Air Terminal, or Hakozaki, if you start your next trip without the proper travel items. This specialty store for the traveler will sell you anything from electric devices (all set up to run on any voltage) to luggage.

42-1 Hakozaki, Nihombashi, Chuo-ku. Hours: 6 a.m.–7 p.m. Tel: 3665-7111.

Best Drug Store

THE AMERICAN PHARMACY, Yurakucho. Americans: many of your favorite drugstore items can be found here, and probably here alone. But this store is American also in its range of products—from candy to vitamins. American prescriptions are filled, as a matter of fact (if validated by a Japanese doctor), and the pharmacist will be glad to recommend a suitable over-the-counter medicine.

1-8-1 Yurakucho, Chiyoda-ku. Hours: 9 a.m.–7 p.m. (11 a.m.–7 p.m. on Sun. & hol.) Tel: 3271-4034. *See Ginza map.*

Best Jewelry Selection

JEWEL PALACE, in the Lumine 2 Department Store in Shinjuku (above the south entrance to Shinjuku Station). Twenty six shops offer the best selection of both costume and fine jewelry at some of the best prices in this city.

1-1-5 Nishi-Shinjuku, Shinjuku-ku. Hours: 11 a.m.–9 p.m. Tel: 3348-5211. *See Shinjuku map.*

Best 50s Stuff

PINK DRAGON, in trendy Shibuya, looks like it just landed from Redondo Beach. James Dean anything, ditto Elvis and Marilyn paraphernalia, ashtrays, toy cars, tube furniture, bags, hats, and clothing, and lots more can be

found in this pink-and-beige, art-deco-style shop. Indeed, the whole building is an art-deco experience. The second floor houses an equally period cafe, complete with Wurlitzer. Cool. Elegant white-on-white Thai restaurant, called Kabala, in the basement (3498-0699).

1-23-23 Shibuya, Shibuya-ku. Hours: 10 a.m.–8 p.m. daily. Tel: 3498-2577. See Aoyama/Harajuku map.

Best Paper Roses

TOKYO-DO, Yotsuya. Three floors of fake flowers you'd swear were real. Artificial flowers on the 1st floor, dried flowers on the 3rd, material and ribbons on the 4th.

2-13 Yotsuya, Shinjuku-ku. Hours: 9:30 a.m.–5 p.m. Closed hol. and 1st & 3rd Sat. & Sun. Tel: 3359-3331.

Best Chinese Junk (with Tea)

DAICHU, Roppongi. It's a nice idea. You can browse among all the funky and inexpensive goods imported from China—tin wind-up toys, cane furniture, great papier-maché masks, Mao suits and hats, coolie shoes, silk pajamas, straw blinds, paper umbrellas, T-shirts, etc.— and then sit down for a bit and enjoy a pot of Chinese tea right there in the store. They offer five kinds of tea and some sweets. Pleasant. Smaller branch on Shibuya's Spain-zaka.

3-16-26 Roppongi, Minato-ku. Hours: 11 a.m.–11 p.m. Tel: 3584-0725. See Roppongi map.

Uchida Bldg. 1F, 16-13 Udagawacho, Shibuya-ku. Hours: 10:30 a.m.–9 p.m. Tel: 3463-8756. See Shibuya map.

Best Artist's Supplies

SEKAIDO, in Shinjuku and other locations. This shop has the largest selection of picture frames, paints, canvases, easels and so on. Comfortably cluttered look, full of artists and artists-to-be. The prices, they claim, are the lowest in town.

3-1-29 Shinjuku, Shinjuku-ku. Hours: 9:30 a.m.–8 p.m. daily. Tel: 3356-1515. *See Shinjuku map.*

Best Used Cameras

MATSUZAKAYA (MAC) CAMERA, near Takanawadai. Main shop has all brands of Japanese cameras—thousands of them, from SLRs to automatic idiot cameras. It's kind of a clearinghouse for cameras that come into pawn shops. One whole floor of Leicas. Least obvious but biggest used camera shop in Tokyo.

1-27-34 Takanawa, Minato-ku. Hours: 10 a.m.–6:30 p.m., until 5 on Sun. & hol. Tel: 3443-1311.

Best Place for Christmas 365 Days a Year

CHRISTMAS COMPANY, Daikanyama. For those who really love Christmas. Everything from tinsel and wrapping paper to mistletoe and stuffed Santas, not just at Christmas but all year round.

Hillside Terrace C-13. 29-10 Sakuragaoka-cho, Shibuya-ku. Hours: 11 a.m.–8 p.m. Closed Mon. unless Christmas is approaching. Tel: 3770-1224.

Best Bathroom with a View

INAX X-SITE, ARK Hills. The very latest in toilet bowls here on the 37th floor. Much more than just a commode shop, Inax provides a sound-and-light show in the foyer, and a video near the information desk about the creative angst of a commode artist as he seeks to conceptualize next year's bowls. Hey, *somebody's* gotta do it. All right, it's easy to make jokes about this place, but after five minutes of chuckling, you find yourself thinking about redoing your own water closet. Amazing exhibition of antique thrones as well.

ARK Mori Bldg. 37F. 1-12-32 Akasaka, Minato-ku. Hours: 11 a.m.–7 p.m. Closed Sun. & hol. Tel: 3505-0311. *See Akasaka map.*

Best New-Idea Goods

OSAMA NO IDEA. It means "the King's ideas," and it's just that. This is a place where unimaginative people can go for their gift shopping. There are 750 novel items on display in this one-small-room shop, ranging from the oddball to the "hey, that's a great idea" variety. Things like swimming goggles for nearsighted people, prism glasses for reading or watching TV while lying down, money belts, funny calculators, telescoping back-scratchers, the world's smallest and lightest umbrella, a bee in a bottle, ultrasonic cockroach repellers, or an electric shoe drier. It's in the bowels of Shinjuku Station, near the elevators (to My City) where two stairways from the underground Marunouchi Line go up to street level across the road from Studio Alta.

3-38-11 Shinjuku, Shinjuku-ku. Hours: 10 a.m.–9 p.m. Tel: 3354-3600. *See Shinjuku map.*

Best Anything

TOKYU HANDS, Shibuya. Please fill in the blanks: You say you need a (_____) that will just fit sideways into your (_____) at home to hold your collection of odd-sized (_____) and (_____), or maybe a (____)-(____) size, extendable (_____) to put in that corner to hold up the (_____) that you will soon buy. At the same time, you don't want to spend your days looking all over town. Tokyu Hands has been a godsend for more than one person trying to set up an apartment in Tokyo and make everything fit. It's the ultimate do-it-yourself store, and a fascinating browse in the bargain. Building supplies from wooden beams to Plexiglas can be cut at the store to your specifications. Hinges, knobs, screws, nails, glues, etc. are available in excess for you to design, build, and finish with. Knock-down furniture helps you fit the furniture to the room. Hobby and craft supplies, scientific apparatus, bathroom and plumbing supplies, kitchen devices and wares, rugs, tiles, and audio and video accessories are just a few of the other things you can find. No ideas on how to improve your place? Just take a stroll through the 21-level Tokyu Hands. You'll have some soon.

12-10 Udagawacho, Shibuya-ku. Hours: 10 a.m.–8 p.m. Closed 2nd & 3rd Wed. Tel: 3476-5461. *See Shibuya map.*

TRADITIONAL SHOPS

Best Traditional Miniature Toys

SUKEROKU, near the Asakusa Kannon in Asakusa. This place should be a delight to those living in doll houses. Sukeroku sells all kinds of miniature figures and toys depicting life during the Edo period. These *gangu*, or toys, are made of wood, clay, or paper, and are quite sought after as souvenirs these days. Problem is, the shop is so small and popular that it's difficult to browse.

2-3-1 Asakusa, Taito-ku. Hours: 10:30 a.m.–6 p.m. Closed Thurs. Tel: 3844-0542. *See Asakusa map.*

Best Sharp Things

MASAMOTO is a little knife shop hard by the Tsukiji Fish Market that will sell you a quality knife for not too high a price, then, as you watch, put an edge on it. You'll have to look for it. Close to the Harumi-Dori side.

4-9-9 Tsukiji. Hours: 6 a.m.–3 p.m. Closed Sun. & hol. and when the fish market is closed.

Best Traditional Dental Aid

Toothpicks, or *yoji*, from **SARUYA**, a shop that has been selling nothing but toothpicks since the Edo period. Needless to say, they offer a wide variety of these little tooth cleaners, most made from *kusunoki* (camphor) wood, noted for its dark color, its fragrance and hardness.

The most popular item is the *senryo bako*, or 1000-*ryo* box, which is considered a good-luck gift, especially at New Year's.

18-10 Koamicho, Nihombashi, Chuo-ku. Hours: 9 a.m.–5 p.m. Closed Sun. & hol. Tel: 3666-3906.

Best Paper Things

WASHIKOBO, Nishi-Azabu. There is something here for everyone. The perfect place for home-bound expats to stock up on thoughtful (and lightweight) little Japanese gifts for anyone that may have been forgotten on the usual

omiyage gift list. The art of Japanese papermaking is displayed in dozens of manifestations—boxes, tea containers, photo albums, decorative wrapping paper, kites large and small, fans ditto, little dainty things, colorful things, precious things. Go in for a glance and you'll stay an hour. There's also a selection of traditional Japanese wooden toys, such as tops and popguns.

1-8-10 Nishi-Azabu, Minato-ku. Hours: 10 a.m.–6 p.m. Closed Sun. & hol. Tel: 3405-1841. *See Roppongi map.*

Best Paper Airplane Supplies

ORIGAMI KAIKAN, Yushima. Everything for the Japanese art of origami, or paper folding. Two floors with more than 1000 kinds of Japanese paper for making dolls, wrapping gifts, crafts, etc.

1-7-14 Yushima, Bunkyo-ku. Hours: 9 a.m.–5 p.m. Closed Sun. & hol. Tel: 3811-4025.

Best Flea Markets

Flea markets in Japan are fun. They have lots of old things for sale, as you would imagine, like chests, writing desks, old household appliances (some rare American or European electric fans, for example), *kimono* and other clothing, dishes, carvings of wood and ivory, *hibachi*, porcelain, prints, and acres more. Also a healthy serving of just junk. But then junkness is in the eye of the beholder. At any rate, these places are great for losing a few hours trying to visualize how that whatchamacallit would look as a planter. You may have seen flea markets in various places in Tokyo, but if you go to a few of them, you'll find that they're mostly the same one, moving around the city. Their schedule is as follows:

1st Sun.: **ARAI YAKUSHI TEMPLE,** *Arai Yakushimae (a short walk from Araiyakushimae Station on the Seibu-Shinjuku Line).* Tel: 3386-1355.

1st & 4th Sun.: **TOGO SHRINE,** *Harajuku.* Tel: 3403-3591. *See Aoyama/Harajuku map.*

2nd Sun.: **NOGI SHRINE,** *Akasaka.* Tel: 3402-2181.

2nd & 3rd Sun.: **HANAZONO SHRINE,** *Shinjuku Sanchome.* Tel: 3200-3093. *See Shinjuku map.*

4th Thurs. & Fri.: **ROPPONGI,** *steps of Roi Bldg.* Tel: 3583-2081. *See Roppongi map.*

If none of these times and locations fit your schedule, drop by the **TOKYO FOLKCRAFT AND ANTIQUE HALL** in Ikebukuro. Thirty-five stalls offering junk to jewels, some American or European, in a very casual flea-market atmosphere. It takes place indoors, so weather is not a concern.

3-9-5 Minami-Ikebukuro, Toshima-ku. Hours: 11 a.m.–7 p.m. Closed Thurs. Tel: 3980-8228.

Best Antique-Shopping Street

The street known as **ANTIQUE KOTTO DORI,** which runs between the Fuji Film Building and Aoyama Dori about a kilometer away, is lined with antique shops that offer items ranging from the souvenir-level to the priceless (except in Japan). Intriguing items not priced out of most people's range can be found at **MORITA GALLERY.**

Morita Gallery: 5-12-2 Minami-Aoyama, Minato-ku. Hours:
10 a.m.–7 p.m., noon–6 p.m. on Sun. & hol. Tel: 3407-4466.
See Aoyama/Harajuku map.

Best One-Stop Antique Store

Not a secret to foreign residents but popular with foreign
visitors is **ORIENTAL BAZAAR**. Touristy, but the place
nonetheless offers some not-so-expensive curios and antiques, large and small. Flower vases, fabrics, kimono,
streamers, china, kites, folding screens, and the like. Give
yourself a break—take your Aunt Martha here when she
visits Tokyo for just two days and wants to buy presents
for 14 people back home.

5-9-13 Jingumae, Shibuya-ku. Hours: 9:30 a.m.–6:30 p.m.
Closed Thurs. Tel: 3400-3933. See Aoyama/Harajuku map.

Best Antique Market

ANTIQUE MARKET, for bargain-free shopping. In the basement of the Hanae Mori Building on Omotesando. Over 30 antique shops, about two-thirds of them dealing in Japanese goods, the others in foreign antiques. The rule of the place is to have one reliable shop for each field of collecting.

3-6-1 Kita-Aoyama, Minato-ku. Hours: 10:30 a.m.–7 p.m. Most shops closed on Thurs. Tel: 3406-1021. *See Aoyama/Harajuku map.*

Best Antique Kimono

HAYASHI KIMONO, Ginza, in the International Arcade.

1-7-23 Uchisaiwaicho, Chiyoda-ku. Hours: 10 a.m.–7 p.m., until 6 p.m. on Sun. Tel: 3591-9825. *See Ginza map.*

Or visit **DAIMARU** Department Store for their sales in February and August, when rental wedding kimono can be had for a song. Check the ads in the dailies for exact dates or call 3212-8011.

Best Japanese Print Sale

COLLEGE WOMEN'S ASSOCIATION OF JAPAN PRINT SHOW AND SALE. Every October, the CWAJ shows over 200 contemporary prints at the Tokyo American Club. Proceeds go to stateside scholarships for deserving Japanese coeds. Call 3583-8381 (Tokyo American Club) to find out when this year's sale will be held.

Best Japanese Crafts Shop

BINGO-YA. Five floors of Japanese folk crafts, or *mingei*, from all parts of Japan. Paper, baskets, ceramics, fabrics, *tansu*, clothing, woodcrafts, lanterns, toys, *kokeshi* dolls, drums, and kites—it's all here. Kind of an upmarket Oriental Bazaar. These *mingei* aren't cheap souvenirs, but often practical things still used in Japan. It's kind of hard to get to, so a taxi from Shinjuku is recommended. Worth the trip.

10-6 Wakamatsucho, Shinjuku-ku. Hours: 10 a.m.–7 p.m. Closed Mon. Tel: 3202-8778.

Best Contemporary Japanese Dolls

AKASAKA SAKURA-DO, Akasaka. Original and unique *kokeshi* (Japanese dolls) for anywhere from a few hundred yen to ¥150,000. Doll designs here are contemporary along classic lines. Check out the scowling *daruma* dolls.

2-5-11 Akasaka, Minato-ku. Hours: 9:30 a.m.–6:30 p.m. (until 3 p.m. on 1st & 3rd Sat.). Closed Sun., hol., 2nd & 4th Sat. Tel: 3586-1546. *See Akasaka map.*

Best Old Folks' Stuff

There's a pedestrian street in **SUGAMO** that caters to the needs of Japan's "Silver" people, kind of a Takeshita-Dori for the elderly. Along the way, you'll find things that you would not in Harajuku—old folks' underwear, medicines, traditional sweets, dried eels (good for what ails you), and the like. At the top of the street is the temple known as Togenuki Jizo. In the courtyard stands a statue, and it is said that if you feel unwell, scrubbing this statue with brush and water on the part that hurts gives you a better chance of recovering. The selling and the scrubbing go on all the time, but especially active are dates with a "4" in them—the 4th, the 14th, and the 24th of the month—

days when the gods are especially attentive to mortal pleas. To get there, take the JR Yamanote Line to Sugamo Station. As you exit the station, look to your right and you will see a street with an arch over it. That's the Sugamo "Silver" street.

Best Traditional Japanese Dolls

KYUGETSU, Asakusabashi. Edo-Dori, near Asakusabashi Station, is lined on both sides with doll and toy shops. Kyugetsu sells traditional Japanese dolls for Girls' Day and Boys' Day, as well as Noh and Kabuki character dolls, pottery dolls, and more. Interestingly, half of the space is now given over to stuffed animals. Need a new 2-meter-tall stuffed Godzilla? There are many toy shops in the area, which used to be mostly for wholesalers but which now sell at retail as well.

1-20-4 Yanagibashi, Taito-ku. Hours: 9:15 a.m.–6 p.m., until 5 p.m. on Sun. & hol. Tel: 3861-5511.

Also good and more accessible for the tourist is **BEISHU CO**. in Ginza.

5-9-13 Ginza, Chuo-ku. Hours: 10 a.m.–5:30 p.m. Closed Sun. & hol. Tel: 3572-1397. *See Ginza map.*

Best Shakuhachi

The *shakuhachi* is the mellow-sounding bamboo flute so prevalent in the music of this country. And it has even been successfully adapted to such non-Japanese types of music as jazz (look for John Kaizan Neptune's recordings). **CHIKUYUSHA** is operated by Junsuke Kawase, a third-generation *shakuhachi* player/teacher/seller/ songwriter/publisher. The flutes cost from ¥10,000 to ¥1,000,000.

3-7 San'eicho, Shinjuku-ku. Hours: 10 a.m.–5 p.m. Closed Sun. & hol. Tel: 3341-5755.

Best Drums

TAIKO-KAN, Asakusa. Drum and bugle, fife and drum, jungle drums—drums of some sort are part of the history of many nations. This is Japan's first museum of drums and only drums. The place has 200 examples of drums from about 80 countries. There are video tapes and books as well, and it's only ¥200 to get in. But what's really cool is that you can play most of them. Take some friends; make some noise. Taiko-Kan is on the 4th floor of Miyamoto Unosuke Shoten. The 1st floor of this building

sells all kinds of festival-related things—costumes, drums, musical instruments, and even *mikoshi*, the portable Shinto shrine that is carried during festival processions.

2-1-1 Nishi-Asakusa, Taito-ku. Hours: 10 a.m.–5 p.m. Closed Mon & Tues. Tel: 3842-5622. See Asakusa map.

Best Extra-Extra-Large Geta

OKADA-YA, Ryogoku. This place has been shoeing large feet for many years, and is now run by Mr. Okano, the third generation of his family to do so. Pick up a large pair of *geta* (wooden sandals) or *zori* (straw sandals). So far the largest sandal they've had to make was for Hawaiian-born sumo wrestler Konishiki (43.5cm). Shops throughout this whole area offer things for sumo wrestlers. The Kokugikan (sumo arena) is nearby as well.

1-17-10 Midori, Sumida-ku. Hours: 9:30 a.m.–8 p.m. (until 6 p.m. on Sun. & hol.). Tel: 3631-2002.

Best Traditional and Not-So-Traditional Tenugui

Tenugui are small, rectangular, cotton cloths used as hand towels or washcloths to scrub (or cover) your body in the bath. Women wear them on their heads when doing housecleaning; men wear them as headbands to absorb sweat or to facilitate concentration (one design sold here has printed on it the cloth's many uses and how to tie it for each use). **FUJIYA** has been in Asakusa for 50 years and is famous for its original and traditional designs. Since many of these head cloths can be considered art, you can also buy them framed. Prices range from ¥800 to ¥10,000.

2-2-15 Asakusa, Taito-ku. Hours: 10 a.m.–8 p.m. Closed Thurs. Tel: 3841-2283. *See Asakusa map.*

And then there's **KAMAWANU** in upmarket Daikanyama, where, in addition to traditional designs, you can find modern patterns or even joke designs, like the one that looks, if tied on your head correctly, like a samurai's *chonmage* hairstyle.

23-1 Sarugakucho, Shibuya-ku. Hours: 11 a.m.–7 p.m. Tel: 3780-0182.

CLOTHING

Best Children's Designer Clothes

PAO, across the street from the TEPCO museum. Kids' merchandising taken to its logical (for Tokyo) extreme. Five floors of everything a kid could want. Fashions are on the fourth floor, kind of like a LaForet for kids. The whole building is overflowing with items to delight the kiddies.

The basement has Kids' Communication: party goods, cooking consultation, personalized knife engraving, and the like. The first floor is stuffed with stuffed animals and dolls. They'll take your picture with a huge stuffed animal for ¥350. Gift-wrapping corner. The second level is for toys, video games, and sports equipment. A toy hospital will do simple repairs. The third is for educational toys, featuring Bornelund, Lego, Pana Kids World (Panasonic electronic educational toys), playground equipment, and a photo shop that will turn your snapshots into posters and T-shirts. Dryer's ice cream.

1-22-14 Jinnan, Shibuya-ku. Hours: 10 a.m.–7 p.m. Closed Wed. Tel: 5458-0111 (switchboard).

Best Children's Clothes

GINZA FAMILIAR, Ginza. Clothe your kid in style at this four-story boutique for the very young, at some very good prices. The sign outside advertises ages "0 to 17," but it's mainly for pre-teens.

6-10-16 Ginza, Chuo-ku. Hours: 11 a.m.–7 p.m. Closed 2nd & 3rd Wed. Tel: 3574-7111. See Ginza map.

Best Designers' Sale

ISETAN, Shinjuku. Twice a year, in January & July, this is the sale that everyone waits for. About 150 men's and women's designer brands, mostly Japanese, are sold at hefty discounts. Members of the store's "I Club" (foreign customers' club) can get an invitation to the pre-sale days, although these days can be just as frenzied. Among the designers available at 30-70 percent discounts are: Issey Miyake, Comme des Garçons, Yohji Yamamoto, Kansai, Kenzo, Zelda, Nicole, and Joseph Tricot.

3-14-1 Shinjuku, Shinjuku-ku. Hours: 10 a.m.–7 p.m. Closed Wed. Tel: 3352-1111. *See Shinjuku map.*

Best 60s Clothes

CHICAGO, Harajuku. The buyers for this basement shop seem to operate on the premise that *somebody* is

going to like this or that rag. Bowling shirts with names like "Chuck" embroidered on the pockets, leather jackets, zoot suits, party dresses your mom (hell, grandmom) could have worn on prom night, hats, emblems, old kimono, and leopard-skin anything.

6-31-21 Jingumae, Shibuya-ku. Hours: 11 a.m.–8:30 p.m. daily. Tel: 3409-5017. *See Aoyama/Harajuku map.*

Best Place for the Latest in Expensive, Japanese Designer Clothing

FROM 1ST, Minami-Aoyama. Situated on a quiet street, this understated collection of boutiques is the first place visiting fashion-minded (read: rich) foreigners head to find the latest in designs by Issey Miyake, Comme des Garçons, Nicole, and others. Below is the relaxed Café Figaro, a favorite fashion-hound hangout. It's a good place for a quiet cup of tea and a bit of shopper-watching.

Café Figaro: 5-3-10 Minami-Aoyama, Minato-ku. Hours: 11 a.m.–11 p.m. daily. Tel: 3499-6786. *See Aoyama/Harajuku map.*

Best Haraju-cutie Store

LAFORET, Harajuku. A "Haraju-cutie" is one of those black-clad children (M or F) that make up a goodly percentage of Japan's fashion-buying public. The initiator of the trend toward boutique-filled buildings, LaForet could be considered the cultural center of Harajuku. That's a little scary. It houses 150 shops on six floors and two basements divided into half levels. Some Japanese designers are represented, but basically it's reasonably priced young fashion. The LaForet Museum on the 5th floor is host to numerous avant-garde events. LaForet Part II, with 50 more shops for the younger-yet generation, is a few blocks north on Meiji-Dori. Look for the lifelike pair of women's legs sticking out of the building.

1-11-6 Jingumae, Shibuya-ku. Hours: 11 a.m.–8 p.m., until 10 p.m. for restaurants. Tel: 3475-0411. *See Aoyama/Harajuku map.*

Best Tailor for Large Outsiders

Any resident football players can get suited up at **LION-DO**, a tailor making suits in sizes as big as you want.

4-30-10 Ryogoku, Sumida-ku. Hours: 9:30 a.m.–6:30 p.m. Closed Sun. & hol. Tel: 3631-0650.

Best Fashion-Boutique Stroll

KILLER DORI is the street that crosses Aoyama-Dori at Bell Commons. It's nearly bursting with fashion in both directions (but heavier on the Bell Commons side), and not all of it in the stores. Most Japanese designers for men and women are represented, and you can find some U.S. preppie stuff and even Western clothes. A good place to watch fashionable people as well, since the denizens more or less make up a continuous fashion parade. But these days, Omotesando has been rapidly catching up. Here, too, both sides of Aoyama-Dori feature *beaucoup* boutiques, but the part to the east of Aoyama-Dori has lately seen the establishment of many Japanese and European designer showrooms. See Aoyama/Harajuku map.

Places

観光

Best Little Piece of the Tropics

Tokyo has replicas of Disneyland, Shakespeare's Globe Theater, Hard Rock Café, and even a replica, you could say, of the Eiffel Tower. If Tokyo were a person, it would be a replica collector. And the latest and most ambitious replica is a replica of a South Pacific island (built on a genuine pile of garbage). It's doubtful if this place will eat into the honeymoon travel trade to real South Pacific islands, but it can't be beat for convenience and a chance for kids to see plants that would never make it through a Tokyo autumn. The **TOKYO-TO YUMENOSHIMA TROPICAL PLANT DOME** sports 4,500 tropical plants in three huge domes (total area: 1500 square meters, highest point: 28 meters), where humidity is maintained at a constant 90 percent and temperature at 25 degrees centigrade (77 degrees Fahrenheit), using waste heat from a nearby industrial plant. It costs ¥200 for adults and high school students, ¥100 for junior high school students, and is free for all others. You shouldn't need to be told this, but stay away on weekends. In fact, 9:30 on a weekday morning would be the best time to enjoy this place. Otherwise it's a four-abreast, Shinjuku Station-style shuffle.

3-2 Yumenoshima, Koto-ku. Hours: 9:30 a.m.– 4 p.m. daily. Closed Mon. Tel: 3522-0281.

Best Hotel Garden

NEW OTANI GARDEN, Akasaka-Mitsuke. This 400-year-old park/garden must have looked quite different in old Tokyo, but it is still a pleasant place to drop by for a relaxing stroll. You needn't be a hotel guest to enjoy it.

The entrance is from the walkway that connects the two towers of the hotel, and signs point the way around the manicured grounds. If you're looking for that classic shot of a lovely, kimono-clad Japanese girl in a perfect setting, hang out for a few minutes by the red bridge one Sunday. New brides and their families often come here to take photographs, and we're sure they wouldn't mind if you snapped a few as well.

4-1 Kioicho, Chiyoda-ku, Hours: 24 hrs./day. Tel: 3265-1111. *See Akasaka map.*

Best Western-Style Garden

SHINJUKU GYOEN, Shinjuku, contains some English- and French-style gardens—separated from the chaos that is Shinjuku by only a fence, but it feels a lot farther away. Be sure to see the orchids in the greenhouse. A nice break, and a great place to read or write letters. Well known for its cherry blossoms and chrysanthemums. Entrance fee is ¥160.

11 Naitocho, Shinjuku-ku. Hours: 9 a.m.– 4 p.m. Closed Mon. Tel: 3350-0151. *See Shinjuku map.*

Best Traditional Parks

KORAKUEN. When most Tokyo residents hear this name, they think of Korakuen Amusement Park, the complex of rides and attractions in the same area. But the name more correctly refers to the adjacent traditional Japanese park. It's among the city's oldest, and certainly among the prettiest. You have a choice of two routes which are outlined on a map near the entrance. We suggest the longer one. You will wind through lush woods, cross bridges (including the "Full Moon Bridge," so called because, being a half-circle over a reflecting pond, its reflection is a complete circle), pass by cherry and plum trees and even glimpse a few symbolic rice paddies. It's a pleasant half-hour walk, and the English-language pamphlet available for purchase at the entrance is a good idea.

1-6-6 Koraku, Bunkyo-ku. Hours: 9 a.m.–4:30 p.m. Hours vary with the season. Tel: 3811-3015.

As were many of the city's gardens, **HAMARIKYU** was, during the Edo era, a private garden, and it maintains an Edo atmosphere. It's natural pond with a bridge is one of Japan's most picturesque. Many birds make their homes among the park's trees, some as old as 300 years, and especially interesting is the colony of *kawau* birds in an isolated corner of the park. More than 1000 of these rare birds can be seen making nests, tending their eggs and young, and feeding. Ask where this area is at the entrance. You can make Hamarikyu your starting point for a trip to Asakusa as boats depart from there as well. Entrance fee is only ¥200. The park is about a 15-minute walk from Shimbashi Station.

1-1 Hamarikyuteien, Chuo-ku. Hours: 9 a.m.–4:30 p.m. Closed Mondays, or Tuesdays when Monday is a holiday. Tel: 3541-0200.

Best Zoo

Unless you count Roppongi Station at 4:30 a.m., before the first train, there is no such thing as a good zoo in Japan.

Best Place to Get Hitched

Well, not really, but a place that must be seen to be believed. **MEGURO GAJYOEN** has been known as a traditional wedding hall for more than half a century, but the old buildings have been torn down and replaced by a huge complex capable of wedding in holy matrimony 60 couples a day. The biggest room can feed 1000 guests buffet-style. But, being "traditional," they have kept the best parts of the old buildings and incorporated them into the new rooms—beams, sculptures, ceilings, etc. Most of

these are on the 4th floor. Go there posing as a happy betrothed couple and walk around. You're free to do so when no one is occupying the rooms. There's a *kaiseki* restaurant, Hosokawa, offering courses from ¥12,000, several other restaurants, a museum housing their collection of Japanese art, a hotel, and a toilet that really has to be experienced featuring a river, bridges, trees, etc. Don't forget to peek into the chapel in the middle of a pond on the roof. But it's not just for weddings, and you can rent any of these rooms for a gathering of any type for prices ranging from ¥20,000 for two hours to ¥2.2 million a day.

1-8-1 Shimo Meguro, Meguro-ku. 8 a.m.–10 p.m. daily. Tel: 3491-4111.

Best Bird Watching

TOKYO-KO YACHO KOEN (Tokyo Bay Bird Park). This place came into being quite naturally (for Tokyo). Years ago, as the area was being reclaimed, some waterfalls were built, and birds began to be attracted to the environment they created. So many that a citizens' group petitioned the Tokyo government to make the place into a sanctuary for birds. This came about in 1986, when it opened as a park. It measures 30 hectares, but, unless you're a bird, you will not be permitted access to all of it. But flightless mammalian bipeds can observe more than 200 kinds of birds from several sites, from small blinds to a three-story structure. It's about a 15-minute walk from the monorail's Ryutsu Center Station. Makes a nice day trip. ¥200 entrance fee.

3-1 Tokai, Ota-ku. Hours 9 a.m.–4:30 p.m. Closed Mon. Tel: 3799-5031.

115

Best Traditional and Socially Approved Excuse for Getting Blasted and Rowdy

If you're under the impression that **CHERRY BLOS-SOM SEASON** is a time for quiet introspection by the nature-loving, sensitive, poetry-writing Japanese, you should take a peek into **UENO PARK** at cherry-blossom time. Acres and acres of wobbling, warbling (generator-powered karaoke sets are not uncommon), average Japanese families or office workers, appreciating nature, sloshed to the gills. Don't just stand there, join in. It isn't difficult to get invited to join one or another group's revelry; indeed, it's a bit difficult to avoid it. Usually around late March. Don't worry, you won't miss it; NHK and other TV stations are nearly obsessive about it, charting the advance of the cherry blossom front as it moves northward from the warmer to the cooler regions of the archipelago.

Best Cherry-Blossom Viewing

AOYAMA BOCHI is a cemetery in the middle of Tokyo. It's a beautiful place at any time of year, but when the cherry blossoms hit Tokyo in April, there are few places to match it. The one-lane road that runs through the cemetery from Nishi-Azabu to Aoyama is breathtaking, transformed as it is into a tunnel of blossoms. The fleeting life of the cherry blossoms (they only last about a week) reminds the Japanese of the transience of all life, so a cemetery is, when you think about it, an especially suitable place to view the blossoms. See Aoyama/Harajuku map.

Best Aoyama/Harajuku Detox Treatment

NEZU PARK, Minami-Aoyama. Boutiqued out? Help is just a few steps farther down Omotesando (on the other side of Aoyama-Dori), a block past the From 1st building. Like most traditional parks, it was once the estate of a nobleman, and it's fun to try to imagine what it must have been like in the past. Teahouses, reflecting ponds, and magnificent stone lanterns await you at every turn. It's hard to believe that this tranquil place is smack in the middle of a usually un-tranquil megalopolis.

6-5-1 Minami-Aoyama, Minato-ku. Hours: 9:30 a.m.–4:30 p.m. Closed Mon. Tel: 3400-2536. See Aoyama/Harajuku map.

Best Cherry-Blossom Lunch

Chinese: **SAIKON** is always a delightful place to have a fine Chinese meal while enjoying the outdoors, and at cherry-blossom time it's even more so. It's atop the hill in Toranomon where the NHK Museum is (and from where Tokyo Rose once broadcast). It's a two-story, wooden, *ryokan*-style place, and a private four-person tatami room on the 2nd floor is recommended. Lunch sets are from ¥1500. Reservations are required for dinner, when courses can be had starting at ¥6000 between 2–10 p.m.

2-1-1 Atago, Minato-ku. Hours: 11:30 a.m.–1:30 p.m., 2–10 p.m. Closed Sun. & hol. Tel: 3437-3618.

French: **LA TERRE**, at the top of the stairs adjacent to the huge Reiyukai Temple in Kamiyacho, has big windows that face the aforementioned stairs, which are covered in an arch of blossoms.

1-9-20 Azabudai, Minato-ku. Hours: 11:30 a.m.–2 p.m., 6–9 p.m. Closed Sun. & hol. Tel: 3583-9682. See Roppongi map.

Best Greenery

TODOROKI, on the Oimachi Line, two stops from Futako-Tamagawaen or three stops from Jiyugaoka Station. You'll be amazed that this much green stuff exists in Tokyo. The 700-meter stroll takes you along the river, below street level. Imagine yourself in another place and time. Start at Todoroki on the marked course along the river that ends at Futako-Tamagawaen. Especially nice in summer. Check out the Nara-period burial mound on the way to Todoroki Fudo Temple.

Best Tiny, Traditional Japanese Amusement Park

HANAYASHIKI, Asakusa. The antithesis of Disneyland, this small place has been delighting people for 130 years. The park, adjacent to the Asakusa Kannon (Sensoji) Temple, is a miracle of low-tech entertainment, from the funky little roller coaster that circles the park to the "rolling room" and the haunted house that you have to grope and feel your way through.

2-28-1 Asakusa, Taito-ku. Hours: 10 a.m.–5 p.m. (until 5:30 on weekends). Closed Tues. Tel: 3842-8780. *See Asakusa map.*

Best Big, Western Amusement Park

TOKYO DISNEYLAND. The ultimate imitation of Western pop art. It's the largest of the four Enchanted Kingdoms but has the smallest parking lot. Concessions have been made for Tokyo's changing climate (covered waiting lines), and for Japan's idea of a day of amusement (visitors are now allowed to bring their own lunches). The easiest way to get there is to take the Keio Line from Tokyo Station to Maihama Station. Basic admission to the park (without rides) is ¥3400 for adults, ¥2300 for children. Advance tickets are usually necessary, especially during the holiday season and on school holidays. The best way to go is to buy the "Passport" (¥4800 adult, ¥3300 children), which gets you in and on all the rides you want.

1-1 Maihama, Urayasu-shi, Chiba-ken. Hours vary with the season, but are usually 9 a.m.– 8 p.m. Mon.–Thurs., 9 a.m.–9 p.m. Fri.–Sun. Tel: 0473-54-0001.

Best Erotic Hill

LOVE HOTEL HILL, Shibuya. For new arrivals, a love hotel is a place where people go to, uh, love. Rooms are rented in two-hour periods (but if you arrive late enough, you can spend the entire night for only a little more). Check-in is done without the desk clerk seeing who is checking in, and even the garage entrance is screened from the street. But love hotels are not just discreet little places to go for a bit of privacy. Not by a long shot. The rooms, you see, go far beyond any normal hotel room in

terms of wanting the customer to enjoy his/her (his/his? her/her? her/his/her?) stay. There's the room with the Ferrari bed, the Hansom cab room, the hall of mirrors, the leather-goddess dominatrix SM torture chamber, and the room where it takes a bit of imagination to figure out just how one is supposed to sit in that chair. What a lot of people don't know is that about half of the couples who use such places are married—to each other. It seems that what with three generations sometimes living in one house, which often has paper walls, a love hotel may be the only place an amorous pair can find privacy. Most places help you in your quest for the ideal room by supplying "picture menus" in the lobby. Also in many lobbies are vending machines (this is, after all, Japan), dispensing what we can only call love paraphernalia. Oh, go ahead. Love hotels are usually recognized by their gaudy signs and occasional castle-motif exteriors. Nowhere is there a greater concentration of this nasty neon and fake stone than on Shibuya's erotic hill, which features little else but love hotels, one after another, in every imaginable fantasy configuration. A stroll through this district is an experience to remember, but don't even bother trying to look innocent. Couples here are hard put to look nonchalant, especially when one is either cajoling or physically pulling the other (it's interesting to note whether the cajoler is the man or the woman). *Hazukashii!* See Shibuya map.

Best Place to Drag the Main

KOEN-DORI, Shibuya, on Friday and Saturday nights (natch). This street, from NHK at one end to Marui on the other, becomes an evening, motorized version of its daytime promenading, young-fashion identity. The funny cars line up and basically go around the block a lot. Exhibiting some confusion about what American style they are emulating at the moment, surf buggies, sports cars, and a surprising number of 4X4s mingle in a cacophony of stereos, powerful engines, and wolf whistles (no, they do not say "hubba hubba"). See Shibuya map.

Best Urban Onsen

AZABU JUBAN ONSEN, Azabu Juban. Right here in the middle of Tokyo is a real onsen (spring-fed bath-house). No, the water does not come out hot; they heat it, but its brownish tint indicates the presence of minerals, which are supposed to be good for you. Soak while enjoying the murals on the walls of the second-floor bath. Little known is the fact that there is a 100-plus tatami-mat party room with a stage on the third floor that can be rented for a small amount for large parties. Food can be arranged, or you may bring your own for a small charge.

1-5-22 Azabu Juban, Minato-ku. Hours: (3F) 11 a.m.–9 p.m. and (1F) 3–11 p.m. Closed Tues. Tel: 3405-4670. *See Roppongi map.*

Best Hotel

HOTEL SEIYO, Ginza. Tokyo has no shortage of good hotels. The Okura, the New Otani, and even the newer Akasaka Prince hotels are known worldwide, but to some they all share a common drawback: the decidedly plebeian circus atmosphere of the lobby of any big, important hotel. Not at the Seiyo. Check-in is done discreetly in a simple, elegantly furnished room. Guest rooms are quiet, furnished in very light pastels, and roomy. Prices are high, starting at about ¥48,000 a night for a single room, and ¥58,000–¥72,000 for a twin. Bustle is non-existent. Bonus: you can obtain the services of a private secretary-cum-concierge, who will smooth your stay in Tokyo.

1-11-2 Ginza, Chuo-ku. Tel: 3535-1111. *See Ginza map.*

Best Look at Japanese Swords

THE JAPANESE SWORD MUSEUM has over 6000 old and new swords (*katana*). One of the first technologies the Japanese excelled in was the art of swordmaking, and the products of the swordmaker's art came to have great cultural significance to the samurai class, a sword being considered a warrior's "soul." The steel was heated and folded repeatedly, creating beautiful, decorative patterns. It's interesting to note that the technology is still practiced today—in the making of sushi knives worth ¥200,000 or more.

4-25-10 Yoyogi, Shibuya-ku. Hours: 9 a.m.–4 p.m. Closed Mon. Tel: 3379-1386.

Best Sword Shop

JAPAN SWORD, Toranomon. Swords from the ancient and genuine (at a cost of one or two million yen) to the dull and fake (for theatrical uses, about ¥10,000). And since swords are not exactly carry-on luggage, they will take care of sending the swords to your home country.

3-8-1 Toranomon, Minato-ku. Hours: 9:30 a.m.–6 p.m. Closed Sun. & hol. Tel: 3434-4321.

123

Best View of Tokyo

Everyone knows about Tokyo Tower, and, what with corporate belt-tightening, the free observation floor atop Mitsui's Kasumigaseki Building has been turned into offices. At 202 meters up, the 45th-floor observation floors of the new **TOKYO CITY HALL** (*Tocho*) are our bet for the best place to look down on the city. There are two of these, one in each of the huge building's two towers, and they're both free, but check to see which ground-floor elevator the tour-bus groups are crowding into and choose the other. For plain opulence, these

observation floors are unexcelled; spacious and with high 18-meter ceilings, they each offer a coffee shop in the center of the room, and kitsch is kept to a minimum. Weather permitting, Mt. Fuji is in plain view, and, except for the opposite tower, the view is 360 degrees.

Hours: 9:30 a.m.–5 p.m. (until 7 p.m. on Sat., Sun. & hol.) Tel: 5320-7890. *Closed Mondays. See Shinjuku map.*

Best Tokyo Skyline

Our last edition had Odaiba, in the middle of Tokyo Bay, as the best place to step back and observe this city's skyline, maybe have a picnic on the grass there. But then they went and built a huge bridge between Odaiba and Shibaura, called "Rainbow Bridge," blocking this fine view. But surprise, when the bridge is opened in the summer of 1993, you can, for a price, walk or maybe even bike across it and get a pretty good view of the city from there. Tokyo looks best from a distance at night. Most cities do.

Best Shinto Shrine

MEIJI SHRINE, Harajuku, is certainly not a secret or at all hard to find. But it's so well known and so convenient that we tend to forget it's Tokyo's most impressive shrine. It offers a pleasant respite from the non-stop pace of all that is Tokyo, and is also a beautiful example of Shinto-style architecture. Enter just across the tracks from Harajuku Station and follow the very wide path under *torii* arches through a man-made, but ecologically self-sustaining (they say), forest to the cedar temple buildings. The

125

serenity is shattered, of course, at New Year's, when, beginning on New Year's Eve, millions (four million in the first three days of the year), visit the shrine to pray for good luck in the new year. And January 15th could be called the most colorful day to visit this temple. That's the day when the country honors all people who have turned 20 in the past year. Young women especially don their best, most colorful kimono and visit the shrine by the thousands. A traditional *momoteshiki* archery competition (shooting from horseback at full gallop) takes place at 1 p.m. nearby.

1-1 Kamizonocho, Yoyogi, Shibuya-ku. Summer hours: 5 a.m.– 6:40 p.m. Winter hours: 6:40 a.m.–4 p.m. (except New Year's). Tel: 3379-5511. *See Aoyama/Harajuku map.*

Best Buddhist Temple

For those who may not know, shrines are dedicated to Japan's ancient, native, polytheistic religion, called Shinto, or "Way of the Gods," while temples are usually Buddhist. Anyway, the best temple, certainly in terms of raw activity and bustle, is **ASAKUSA KANNON (SENSOJI)**, Asakusa. The temple was built in the eighth century to enshrine a small statue of Kannon, the Buddhist goddess of mercy, which fishermen found nearby. In marked contrast to the peaceful order and aesthetic beauty of Meiji Shrine, this raucous place is a three-ring circus of the dutifully faithful of Tokyo. Incense stalls fill the area with fragrant smoke as thousands of visitors swarm through the huge gates and along the main street of souvenir stands on their way to the main temple building. There the crowds are often so thick that you must throw your coins over the heads of a dozen people to hit the offerings box. On festival days

(Sanja Matsuri in mid-May), just multiply the above description by two or three. In ancient times, this was one of the city's liveliest areas (the famed Yoshiwara pleasure quarter was a few blocks north), and it remains the place to go for a taste of how the working-class Japanese kick back.

2-3-1 Asakusa, Taito-ku. Hours: 6:30 a.m.–5 p.m. Tel: 3842-0181. *See Asakusa map.*

Best Indoor Spaces

SPIRAL, Aoyama. In a city that gives so little attention to exteriors and so much to interiors, it's difficult to call one or two indoor areas the best. But Spiral makes use of lots of what is probably, due to its scarcity, Tokyo's most valuable building material: space. Designed by Maki Fumihiko, Spiral offers an open lobby café where you can

sit and feel the luxury of nothingness around you. Sip a cup of coffee or try the Sunday brunch (popular with a certain trendy crowd, but actually just so-so), from 11 a.m. to 2 p.m. for ¥3500. On two sides of the café is a gallery with monthly shows that often seem expressly designed for the space, which consists of a wide concourse and a huge, circular, skylit, open area with a ramp that takes the viewer gradually up to the second-floor gift shop.

5-6-23 Minami-Aoyama, Minato-ku. Hours: 11 a.m.–8 p.m. Tel: 3498-1171. See Aoyama/Harajuku map.

MANIN, Harajuku. The entrance way to this three-story, Philip Starck-designed underground cavern is as impressive as the entrance you will make, descending down two floors of black marble stairs in full view of the high dining room. (Watch your step; the altitude is somewhat dizzying, and you don't want your entrance to be more impressive than it has to be.) The cave-like atmosphere is heightened by the directional lights shining straight down on each table from nine meters above. Expensive, of course.

Manin Bldg. B1. 2-22-12 Jingumae, Shibuya-ku. Hours: 6–10:45 p.m. Closed Sun. Tel: 3478-3081. See Aoyama/ Harajuku map.

The lobby of **SOGETSU KAIKAN**, Aoyama Dori. Changing, imaginative decorations, flowers, and waterfalls make this Tange-designed lobby a wonderful contrast to the bustle of Tokyo outside. Next door to the Canadian Embassy.

7-2-2 Akasaka, Minato-ku. Tel: 3408-1126. See Akasaka map.

Best Industrial Showrooms/ Buildings

TEPCO, Shibuya. TEPCO (the Tokyo Electric Power Company) has built a fun place for children and adults alike. Hands-on, interactive exhibits on the generation and use of electric power, video editing rooms, word processors to use, an art gallery, a coffee shop, and even cooking classes. Free movies on Monday afternoons. English brochure and captions add to the enjoyment.

1-12-10 Jinnan, Shibuya-ku. Hours: 10:30 a.m.–6 p.m. Closed Wed. Tel: 3477-1191. *See Shibuya map.*

THE MUSEUM OF TOBACCO & SALT, Shibuya. Whether you smoke or not, the M of T & S offers some good exhibits of smoking devices from as far back as the Edo period. How about salt sculptures? Actually the jewel here is a quiet coffee shop that offers a respite from the manic merchandising of Shibuya.

1-16-8 Jinnan, Shibuya-ku. Hours: 10 a.m.–6 p.m. Closed Mon. Tel: 3476-2041. *See Shibuya map.*

SONY BUILDING, Ginza. Of course, most manufacturers and all electronics manufacturers have such showrooms, but Sony's layout, combined with their technological adventurism, makes for some electronics marvels you may not have seen yet. In a stepped floor arrangement, the visitor gets to see and play with many of the company's best and newest products, from shortwave radios and car stereos to projection televisions and exhibits of the newest-of-the-new high-definition television (HDTV) that Sony has had a hand in developing. A special exhibit of export models (that won't necessarily

129

work in Japan) is a plus for bewildered tourists wondering what will work back home.

5-3-1 Ginza, Chuo-ku. Hours: 11 a.m.–7 p.m. Tel: 3573-2371. See Ginza map.

HONDA SHOWROOM, Aoyama Itchome. A biker's dream. Many of the latest sports motorcycles, scooters, factory choppers, and dirt bikes. Sit on 'em. Take her off the stand and imagine the open road (not easy in this city). Usually spicing things up a bit is one of the Honda F1 race cars that are winning worldwide these days, and some of the company's newest cars, like the 4-wheel-steering Prelude.

2-1-1 Minami Aoyama, Minato-ku. Hours: 9:30 a.m.–6:30 p.m., 10 a.m.–6 p.m. Sat., Sun. & hol. Tel: 3423-4118.

AMLUX is Toyota's huge new six-floor arena for displaying its new cars. You can browse among concept cars, take in a short film, see how Toyotas are built, be amazed by

F1 and other racing cars, or just inspect this year's white four-door.

3-3-5 Higashi Ikebukuro (near Sunshine 60), Toshima-ku. Hours: 11 a.m.–8 p.m. (10 a.m.–7:30 p.m. on Sun. & hol.) Closed Mon. Tel: 5391-5900.

Best Children's Castle

CHILDREN'S CASTLE, Aoyama (*Kodomo no Shiro*). More correctly referred to as the National Children's Center, this complex with the somewhat frightening sculpture in front houses a swimming pool (open to adults), a theater hall, an audio-visual library, and hands-on video camera and computer areas. The castle plans and organizes events for children.

5-53-1 Jingumae, Shibuya-ku. Hours: 12:30–5:30 p.m. (10 a.m.–5:30 p.m. on weekends & hol.). Closed Mon. Tel: 3797-5666. *See Aoyama/Harajuku map.*

Best Planetarium

GOTO PLANETARIUM AND ASTRONOMICAL MUSEUM, Shibuya. Different shows each month on the planets, stars, sun, and moon, projected by a Zeiss projector onto a 20-meter dome. Saturday from 6 p.m. features a special evening with various kinds of music. Changes every month. Entrance ¥800 adult, ¥500 children.

Tokyu Bunka Kaikan, 2-21-12 Shibuya, Shibuya-ku. Hours: 10 a.m.– 6 p.m. Mon.–Fri., 10:30 a.m.–6 p.m. Sat., Sun. & hol. (Hours change with the season, please call before going.) Tel: 3407-7409. *Closed Mon. See Shibuya map.*

Best Architectural Galleries

GA GALLERY, Sendagaya. Home of the international architecture magazine A.D.A. EDITA. Each room is unique. This is the place for students of Japan's post-modern architecture to go for books on the subject.

3-12-14 Sendagaya, Shibuya-ku. Hours: 10 a.m.–6 p.m. Closed weekends & hol. Tel: 3403-1581.

POCKET PARK is a comfy little spot run by Tokyo Gas in Ginza. The ground floor has regular exhibits on Japanese architecture, usually featuring interesting architectural models and drawings. The second floor has more exhibits and a long wall of books and magazines on architecture, some in English.

7-9-15 Ginza, Chuo-ku. Hours: 10:30 a.m.–7 p.m. Closed Wed. Tel: 3573-1401. *See Ginza map.*

Best No-Frills Japanese Garden Party

KIYOSUMI GARDEN was once the estate of a rich Edo-period merchant. In it are ponds, rocks, paths, and a little house beside the lake. As many as 40 people can fit into the house, and you can rent it for three-and-a-half hours in the morning, afternoon, or evening for only ¥4,600—and talk about bargains, that's for the *whole place*, not per person. It belongs to the ward, so there are the inevitable regulations, and you must plan a month in advance. Arrangements can be made for modest, *obento*-style meals. Call 3641-5892 for details or write 3-3-9 Kiyosumi, Koto-ku. Open 9 a.m.–4:30 p.m.

Best Concentration of Today's Youth

TAKESHITA-DORI, running between the north exit of Harajuku Station and Meiji-Dori. If Harajuku is known for its teeny-bopper crowd, Takeshita-Dori is younger than young. This amazing, trendy little street is always packed with squealing, babbling Japanese kids having fun. It's especially jammed on weekends since, to youths from the sticks (here that's Chiba and Saitama prefectures), a trip to Harajuku is the perfect Sunday thing to do. (*"Yaaadaaa!" "Uso!" "Eeeeeeeehhh?"*) See Aoyama/Harajuku map.

Best Cemetery

AOYAMA BOCHI. Look at it on a map and it's hard to resist the instincts of a realtor: over a quarter million square meters of prime, mid-city Tokyo land, and not a living soul. For sheer prestige, Aoyama Cemetery (officially Aoyama Reien but better known as Aoyama Bochi) is the address to end all addresses. Most renowned of the *bochi's* residents is the hero of the Russo-Japanese War, General Maresuke Nogi (1849–1912), buried just a few minutes' walk from his old home in Nogizaka. Most visited grave, however, is probably Naoya Shiga's (1883–1971), a novelist immensely popular in his own day and still idolized by young literary types. Grandest of the graves belongs to Meiji politico Toshimichi Okubo (1830–1878). The calligraphy on this huge monolith of a monument is considered one of the finest examples of its era. The tombstone can be found nearby, mounted on the back of a giant stone turtle. The sentimental favorite is Hachiko (1922–35), the loyal hound of Shibuya Station, reunited here at last with his beloved master. But these are only the best known. With some 110,000 recorded burials since it opened in 1874, the *bochi* represents a cross section of the famous, the infamous, and the unknown from the Meiji, Taisho, and early Showa eras. One section was set aside for police officers killed in the line of duty. Elsewhere are soldiers from half a dozen campaigns, generations of Kabuki actors, and bank presidents with tombs in the shape of giant coins. Surprisingly unpublicized is the foreigners' cemetery; suddenly in the midst of Shinto lanterns and Buddhist icons, you begin to come upon crosses and slab tombstones. Like the foreigners' cemetery in Yokohama, this one is devoted largely to resident Europeans and North Americans who contributed to the Meiji Restoration: teachers, journalists, doctors, scientists, and engineers. Here lie men and women who helped Japan build waterworks and ships and railroads, send telegraphs, process food, fight infectious disease. One Englishman is on record as having taught the Japanese the exotic new art of making Western-style shoes. An Italian artist buried here is remembered as having helped the Meiji government design its stamps and money. Much of the interest here derives from the variety of the graves themselves—a virtual survey of European burial customs. Nor are Christian graves limited to foreigners. In best Meiji tradition, Aoyama Cemetery was from the beginning open to all faiths. Its last famous burial, in fact, was that of a Japanese Christian, post-war Prime Minister Shigeru Yoshida (1878–1967). What has become a limiting factor, however, is space. In 1960 the Tokyo metropolitan government announced an end to all new plots in all public cemeteries (of which this is one) within the city's 23 wards. Mr. Yoshida himself wouldn't have been allowed in if his family hadn't purchased a plot in the cemetery over half a century before. And the fate of this lovely, sun-dappled (and almost priceless) piece of land? That remains in the hands of the city's planners, who have announced nothing yet and appear in no hurry to do so. But it seems clear that Aoyama Cemetery has become simply too precious a piece of property to let rest in peace. One idea is to build a pavilion with another complete layer of graves above or below the present one. Similar multistory arrangements have been used at other cemeteries in Japan. Another possibility is to transport the entire cemetery, stone by stone, urn by urn, to some distant suburb. Aoyama Cemetery will almost surely survive, if not necessarily in Aoyama.

—John Kennerdell

Best Police Box

Police boxes, or *koban*, are mini police stations scattered throughout Japan's cities that house from two or three to twenty or more (in entertainment districts) "neighborhood policemen." It's a system many Western cities have tried to emulate (San Francisco has established quite a few trial *koban*). The police officers sit on duty in their police box and assist callers and patrol the surrounding area on foot or bicycle. Graduates fresh out of police school are always assigned to *koban* duty. Lately, Tokyo has been dressing up some of the *koban* in areas heavily frequented by tourists. One of the best known is the **GINZA**

SUKIYABASHI POLICE BOX. But the knights in this red brick castle (designed by Kazumasa Yamashita) at Sukiyabashi intersection are blue-uniformed *omawari-san*. This, by the way, is also the busiest police box in the country; not for crimes—for giving directions.

4-1-2 Ginza, Chuo-ku. Hours: Ever alert. See Ginza map.

Another eye-catching *koban* on the cutting edge of cop-box design (you'd have to see it) is in Shibuya, about halfway up the street that runs from Seibu Department Store to Tokyu Hands. Designed by architect Edward Suzuki.

Best Magazine Browsing

MAGAZINE HOUSE, Higashi-Ginza. There's nothing wrong with hanging out at a bookstore in this country reading magazines you have no intention of buying. It's acceptable behavior. As a foreigner, though, you may run through the available magazines in your language rather rapidly. Boy, is there a place for you! The Magazine House has this month's edition of over 1100 magazines from 40 countries. (You are not allowed to check out the magazines, but there's a great sale of back issues about every six months.) You can take your selections to the adjacent coffee shop and enjoy your magazine over a cup of great spice tea. An article you'd like to keep? There's a coin-operated copier on the premises. It's the big pink-and-gray building with Popeye and Olive on the doors, a block behind Kabuki-za in Higashi-Ginza.

3-13-10 Ginza, Chuo-ku. Hours: 11 a.m.–7 p.m. Closed weekends & hol. Tel: 3545-7227. See Ginza map.

Best Look at What Tokyo Used to Be

SHITAMACHI MUSEUM, Ueno Park. You know that Tokyo wasn't always like this, and that at one time in history things were simpler. You've read about the *shitamachi* (old downtown; "below the castle walls") area of Tokyo, and even tried to catch glimpses of it in Asakusa/Ueno. This museum makes it easy to picture what it was like back then, with sample houses, conveyances, craft demonstrations, photos, and prints.

2-1 Ueno, Taito-ku. Hours: 9:30 a.m.–4 p.m. Closed Mon. Tel: 3823-7451.

Best Old Tokyo Neighborhood

In Nippori, explore a bit around the **YANAKA** area to find some fine examples of *nagaya*, old-style, connected wooden houses, which you see these days only in samurai films. Many small temples are in the area, as well as a famous cemetery. A good walking course starts at Nippori Station (Yamanote Line). First stop is Yanaka Cemetery with its five-story pagoda and Buddha statue. Look at the tea houses in the cemetery where tired mourners go to catch a breather and a cuppa. Next, go to **Asakura Chosokan,** once the studio and home of famed sculptor Asakura Fumio. It's nominally a sculpture museum, and Mr. Asakura's works are dutifully on display here. But more than that, it's one of this area's best-preserved traditional Japanese houses. It surrounds a small spring-fed pond and garden, and each room holds a surprise or two. Pay attention to the details here: the special woods used, the use of bamboo, the *shoji* paper screens. (Admission ¥300. 7-18-10 Yanaka, Taito-ku. Hours 9:30 a.m.–

4:30 p.m. Closed Monday and Friday. Tel: 3821-4549).
Yanaka is where the row houses are. There are almost 70
in this area. Do a bit of *zazen* (meditation) at **Zenshoan,**
where former Prime Minister Nakasone used to settle his
nerves. Open 5–9 a.m. (Tel: 3821-4715) Famed for its
collection of ghost paintings. Hmm. Next is **Daimyo
Dokei Hakubutsukan** (Hours: 9 a.m.–4 p.m., Tel:
3821-6913)—old-style clock museum with antique
timekeeping devices, sundials, etc. Finish the walk at
Sendagi Station on the Chiyoda Line.

Best Post-50s, International Contemporary Art Museum

HARA MUSEUM, Shinagawa. Art-deco building, a garden, sculptures, outdoor exhibits. Also organizes bilingual lecture-and-video series in English several times a year. A yearly membership (¥10,000) gets you a quarterly newsletter, invitations to opening parties, and free entrance for yourself and your guests. Entrance fee: ¥600.

4-7-25 Kita-Shinagawa, Shinagawa-ku. Hours: 11 a.m.–5 p.m., until 8 p.m. on Wed. Closed Mon. Tel: 3445-0651.

Best Historical Museum

KAIGAKAN (Meiji Memorial Picture Gallery). The main attraction in this piece of epic architecture adjacent to the Jingu Kyujo baseball stadium is a large mural made up of 80 panels depicting Japan's modern history, from feudal times through the Meiji Restoration. The steps are also a good place to sun oneself on nice days. The building itself is naturally cool in summer, frigid in winter.

9 Kasumigaoka, Shinjuku-ku. Hours: 9 a.m.–4 p.m. daily. Tel: 3401-5179. *See Aoyama/Harajuku map.*

Best Museum Area

UENO PARK. Japan's parallel to the British Museum or the Smithsonian, Ueno Park houses an awesome array of treasures: the Tokyo National Museum (Japanese art and archaeology), Tokyo Metropolitan Art Museum (Japanese crafts, prints, sculpture), the National Science Museum (a rather uninspired effort for a technological giant), the National Museum of Western Art (painting and sculpture from the Renaissance on), and more.

Tokyo National Museum: 13-9 Uenokoen, Taito-ku. Hours: 9 a.m.–4:30 p.m. Closed Mon. Tel: 3822-1111/7.

Best Museum-as-Art

TOKYO-TO TEIEN MUSEUM. This beautiful art-deco building, the former residence of Prince Asaka, is often more interesting to view than the loaned exhibitions it offers. Nice lawn and park area complete with ducks, too.

5-21-9 Shiroganedai, Minato-ku. Hours: 10 a.m.–5:30 p.m. Closed 2nd & 4th Wed. Tel: 3443-0201.

Best Kitsch

TOKYO TOWER SOUVENIR SHOPS. Stall upon crowded stall of tower models, Godzilla puppets, tacky lighters, glowing things, noisy things, cute things, and completely dumb things. While you're checking out the kitsch, watch the visitors who are buying the stuff.

4-2-8 Shibakoen, Minato-ku. Hours: 9 a.m.–6 p.m (until 7 p.m. on weekends & hol.). Tel: 3433-5111. See Roppongi map.

Best Rendezvous Spots

Getting around Tokyo is easier with a guide, someone who has been here for a bit and can take you in tow. But

141

meeting up with him/her is often the first and most difficult step. The following few places are traditionally designated as rendezvous spots. Everyone in the respective areas knows where they are and will direct you (if not deliver you) to them if you get lost.

Roppongi

ALMOND (Amando). Probably the first place anyone coming to Japan is likely to have to find. And it's not

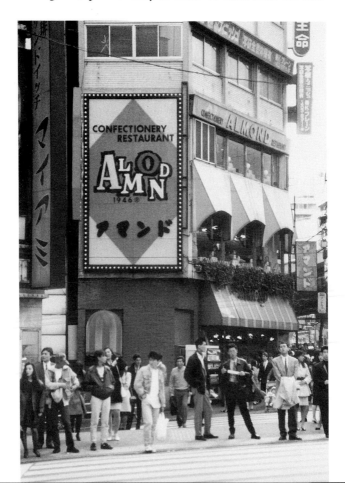

difficult, seeing as this corner coffee shop is bright pink, with white stripes. As you leave Roppongi Station through the main exit (the one away from Hiro-o, toward Kamiyacho, not the one near the WAVE building), Almond is nearby. If you come up on the wrong side of the street, just look for a lot of shocking pink. Just to be clear, the recommended rendezvous spot is outside the building. No guidebook in its right mind would recommend that you actually enter this mediocre place. See Roppongi map.

Shibuya

HACHIKO. The statue of that obsessive-compulsive dog is perhaps the country's best-known, fabled even, meeting place. You'll have to pick out the person you are to meet from the thousands of others there for the same purpose, but it is easy to find. Hint: arrange to meet at the police box near Hachiko; it's just a bit less crowded. See Shibuya map.

Shinjuku

STUDIO ALTA. On the east side of the station on Shinjuku-Dori is a building that looks like a giant TV screen, which is exactly what it is. The place to meet is out front, under the big tube. Hint: arrange to meet across the street in the "green" space in front of the station; you feel less crowded and can watch the screen. See Shinjuku map.
KINOKUNIYA BOOKSTORE, street level. Also a covered spot. If you're early you can browse through the sixth floor foreign-language books. Near Isetan, Mitsukoshi, and Golden Gai. See Shinjuku map.
SOUTH EXIT, SHINJUKU STATION (Shinjuku Eki, Minami-guchi) for those times you are meeting in Shinjuku to start a train trip. See Shinjuku map.

143

Aoyama

BELL COMMONS. Fashionably situated on the corner of Aoyama Dori and the boutique-infested "Killer Dori," Bell Commons is itself a collection of boutiques. Anyway, it's visible. Near every designer-brand shop Japan has ever spawned. See Aoyama/Harajuku map.

Akasaka

BELLE VIE. Where better to meet someone in Akasaka than at the top of the escalators of Akasaka-Mitsuke subway station's main exit? The breezeway through this fashion building is covered and the people-watching is great. See Akasaka map.

Ginza

WAKO. Out for a little shopping, ladies? You can't miss Wako, smack in the middle of some of the planet's most expensive real estate. The stone building (1932) and its clock tower have long been roughly equal to the clock at Grand Central Station as a rendezvous spot. While you're waiting for your late friend, enjoy the unique, often mechanized window displays, or just gaze at the passing parade. Near all the Ginza department stores and shops. See Ginza map.

SONY BUILDING, Ginza. Right above Ginza Station and within a stone's throw of Yurakucho Station, perhaps ten movie houses, a few hundred restaurants, the Press Club, and the Tourist Information Center, the Sony Building is a particularly good place to meet on a rainy day (you can wait inside). See Ginza map.

Tokyo Station

The **GIN NO SUZU** (silver bell) meeting area at the central exit of Tokyo Station, Yaesu side.

Best New-Religion Edifice

That football-field-sized object in Kamiyacho that looks like it just arrived from Klingon is the **REIYUKAI**, headquarters of the Buddhist sect of the same name. You can go inside if you ask at the visitor center at the entrance, where you can pick up a leaflet in English. The huge interior space wondrously echoes the chanting of the as many as 5000 followers, mostly old ladies.

1-7-8 Azabudai, Minato-ku. Hours: 6 a.m.–5 p.m. Closed Wed. Tel: 5563-2520. *See Roppongi map.*

Best One-Day Art Trip out of Tokyo

MOA MUSEUM, Atami. It's a great museum, architecturally as well as artistically. The entrance to the mountaintop museum building is via four huge escalators

145

through the bottom of the mountain. The bottom of the mountain is reached via a free shuttle from Atami Station, which is in turn reached in only an hour via Shinkansen Kodama (the slower speeding bullet) from Tokyo Station, and we assume you can find that. The museum is run by a group connected with the Church of World Messianity. It's a crowd-free, nearly foolproof day trip for people who get lost easily. That, by the way, also makes it ideal as a destination for those visitors from home that you don't have time to entertain. On view are three Cultural Treasures, 53 Important Cultural Properties, a fine collection of Japanese and Chinese art, a replica of Hideyoshi's golden tea room, a Noh theater, and monthly art exhibits. After taking in all this, you can stroll the seaside town of Atami (poke your head into the little amusement park in summer), and have some very fresh sashimi at any of the many small restaurants. The park behind Atami Station, by the way, is famed for its plum blossoms, which come out about a month before the cherry blossoms do, usually in February.

26-2 Momoyamacho, Atami-shi, Shizuoka-ken. Hours: 9:30 a.m.–4:30 p.m. Closed Thurs. Tel: 0557-84-2511.

Best High

Few people know that you can rent the entire **UPPER OBSERVATION DECK OF TOKYO TOWER** for a party. You must get together a minimum of 100 people, and no more than 200, to do it. It's available from mid-November to mid-March on weekdays, 6:30–8:30 p.m., and will cost about ¥10,000 per person including food and drink. Call 3433-5111 (in Japanese, please) if you really think you want to do this.

Entertainment

娯

楽

Best Pure Theater

KABUKI, of course. Noh may be beautiful and poetic, but Kabuki is *theater*. With dazzling costumes, dramatic plots, movable platforms, and flying actors, Kabuki seldom fails to entertain. Tokyo's two venues for Kabuki are both great: **KABUKI-ZA** is, of course, devoted to nothing else, while the **NATIONAL THEATER** offers Kabuki and other entertainments. See *Tokyo Journal* for information on monthly offerings.

Kabuki-za: 4-12-15 Ginza, Chuo-ku. Tel: 3541-3131. *See Ginza map.*

*National Theater (*Kokuritsu Gekijo*): 4-1 Hayabusacho, Chiyoda-ku.* Tel: 3265-7411.

Best Movie Theaters

Long-time residents of Tokyo remember what an excruciating experience it once was to take in a movie here. Most complaints stemmed from the size of the seats (tiny, little legroom). The newer theaters have alleviated this complaint, but it's still a bit of a crush to get a seat at a popular film with the Japanese habit of crowding in before the feature is over and jumping for vacated seats. By and large, the newer houses, like Piccadilly, Louvre, Nihon Gekijo in the Mullion (Yurakucho Center) Building, and the new Hibiya Chanter complex, have solved the small-seat problem, with large, comfortable seats and pleasing surroundings. Some theaters are shows in themselves, such as the astoundingly designed **CINEMA RISE** in Shibuya.

Rise Bldg. 13-17 Udagawacho, Shibuya-ku. Tel: 3464-0052. *See Shibuya map.*

Late Shows

HAIYU-ZA CINEMA 10, in Roppongi, offers late shows starting at 9:45 p.m. nightly. Cinema 10 avoids popular blockbusters in favor of smaller, quality pictures in both English and other non-Japanese languages, and the mob scene is largely avoided here, although the theater can fill up quickly on Friday and Saturday nights.

4-9-2 Roppongi, Minato-ku. Tel: 3470-2880. *See Roppongi map.*

Foreign Films

CINE VIVANT, Seibu's class-act theater in the WAVE Building, shows selected European films and the occasional "art" film in English. And like Haiyu-za Cinema 10 above, Cine Vivant offers late shows.

WAVE Bldg. B1. 6-2-27 Roppongi, Minato-ku. Tel: 3403-6061. *See Roppongi map.*

Traditional Japanese Movies

NAMIKIZA. Really old but fun. Frequently, monthly series are shown. This funky little place in Ginza is nearly a shrine to old Japanese movies, movie stars, and directors.

2-3-5 Ginza, Chuo-ku. Tel: 3561-3034. *See Ginza map.*

Best Juke Box

GEORGE'S BAR, on a little corner of the *Boeicho*, Japan's Defense Ministry in Roppongi, has been in the same place for over 25 years. George's is a favorite of recording-industry types, both domestic and visiting. The walls are bedecked with posters, album covers, and autographs of R&B greats, and the venerated, low-tech jukebox rumbles away for hours on end, playing James Brown, Wilson Pickett, the Temptations, and other soulful names. We once figured out that George (who happens to be a woman) has heard "My Girl" approximately 145,000 times since she first plugged in this wondrous juke box. You can't get there early, because George doesn't even unlock the front door until 9 p.m., but you can stay late, because she leaves it open until 7 a.m. or later if she still has customers.

9-7-55 Akasaka, Minato-ku. 9 p.m.–7 a.m. daily. Tel: 3405-9049. *See Roppongi map.*

Best Live Music

This is not New York or Chicago, where you can go hit any of a number of jazz or rock clubs and be assured of a good evening of music. In jazz, for instance, the names that play regular gigs in the U.S. are concert acts here; bring your binoculars. There are, however, a number of what are called "live houses." Check *CityScope* (in *Tokyo Journal*) or the dailies for a list of concerts and live clubs. Clubs range from the funky to the high-class and high-cost.

Ethnic, folk, salsa, etc.

CAY, in the basement of the Spiral Building on Aoyama Dori, offers some great ethnic music performances. It's a Thai restaurant when there isn't live music.

5-6-23 Minami-Aoyama, Minato-ku. Hours: 6 p.m.–midnight. Closed Sun. & hol. Tel: 3498-5790. *See Aoyama/ Harajuku map.*

151

Class Acts

BLUE NOTE, Aoyama. This room offers the best of both worlds for the jazz fan. Turned off by ¥6000 baseball-stadium concerts where the giant TV screens give you the only glimpse of the performers? Equally turned off by the ¥20,000-plus tariff required to see big-name jazz artists at hotel dinner shows? Jazz aficionados will find that the Blue Note offers the more intimate venue (200 seats) necessary for full enjoyment of good jazz. It costs ¥7000–¥10,000 to get in, but, to many, the chance to see the likes of Tony Bennett, Sergio Mendes, Jon Hendricks, or Joe Williams, up close, is worth it. Japanese jazz fans won't blink at the price. Two shows each night, usually at 7:30 and 10. The club is a franchise (the first of many planned for the U.S. and Europe), and an exact copy of the successful Blue Note in New York.

5-13-3 Minami Aoyama, Minato-ku. Tel: 3407-5781. *See Aoyama/Harajuku map.*

Asian, Indian, Arab, etc.

RAUYA was specializing in Asian, Indian, and Arab music long before the somewhat Japlish term "ethnic" came into vogue. The small space seats only 50 or so, with a tiny stage along one wall. Small dolls, toys, and curios decorate the place. The food is mainly curries from various countries, cooled a bit from their original fieriness, complemented by drinks like Indian masala tea, hibiscus tea, and Haitian coffee. About three times a week they offer live music—Indian classic and movie music, Caribbean, Okinawan, Eastern European, South American, African, popular and even a bit of Chicago blues. Check their live music schedule. Shows are usually at 7 and 9:30, and the music charge is ¥1500–¥2000. They also organize music lessons, mainly for percussion instruments, at **MINZOKU**

ONGAKU CENTER, or Folkloric Music Center, where lessons on a variety of Asian, African, and Caribbean percussion instruments are offered—*tabala, dholak, daf, doira, jembe, lunga* talking drum, maracas, *oud, saz,* and *darbuka*. Also Greek and Indian instruments and music. Both places are five minutes from Kichijyoji Station. Call 0422-47-5726 for information.

B1 Yayoi Bldg., 1-8-11 Kichijyoji Minami, Musashino-shi. Tel: 0422-46-8533

No-nonsense Jazz

The PIT INN in Roppongi & Shinjuku. The cover, usually ¥3000, includes a drink. Relaxed, even funky atmosphere allows you to focus on the quality artists booked here. Roppongi leans toward fusion and a variety of other acts, and the Shinjuku location concentrates on straight jazz.

3-17-7 Roppongi, Minato-ku. Hours: 6:30–10 p.m. Tel: 3585-1063. *See Roppongi map.*

Accodo Shinjuku B1, Shinjuku 2-chome, Shinjuku-ku. Hours: 2–4:30 p.m., 7–11 p.m. Tel: 3354-2024. *See Shinjuku map.*

Best Echo Chamber

NIHON BUDOKAN. Built in 1964 as the martial arts arena for the Tokyo Olympics, this is one of the best and best-looking buildings for that purpose. But stay away from it for concerts, as most acts, unless you're near the sound system, sound like they are being performed in a sewer.

2-3 Kitanomaru Koen, Chiyoda-ku. Tel: 3216-5100.

Best Sleaze Pickup Bar

Somebody here has to mention **CHARLESTON**, if only because it has remained virtually unchanged over the years, except downward. Unchanged and only seldom (and never successfully) challenged as Roppongi's best dive. Some nights you can count more cockroaches than customers, and other nights it's not so crowded. Feel as though you're at the bottom of the *gaijin* pit here and need a boost? Hanging out at Charleston until it closes some night is the best inspiration toward self-improvement we've ever exper...uh, heard about. But establishments are defined by their clientele, and Charleston's after-midnight crowd is especially crude, starring numerous GIs, with their famed thirst for cultural understanding, semi-pro athletes, middle-aged foreign businessmen, who drink in ties, some very strange Japanese, and best of all, the huntresses, desperate girls who find these types attractive.

3-8-11 Roppongi, Minato-ku. Hours: 6 p.m.–5 a.m. daily. Tel: 3402-0372. *See Roppongi map.*

Best Entertainment Information

TOKYO JOURNAL'S CITYSCOPE section. Aside from the fact that the authors of this book have both in the past had something to do with this publication, *CityScope* really is the only English publication where you'll find a full month of entertainment information, all in one place. Schedules for art, film, music, performing arts, festivals, and events are included, with short articles and recommendations in each department. Pick up a copy of *Tokyo Journal* (to get *CityScope*) at any bookstore or call the office.

Emphasis! Central Roppongi Bldg. 4F, 1-4-27 Roppongi, Minato-ku. Tel: 3585-6377.

Best Discos

In the opinion of many, a "good disco" is a contradiction in terms. The mindless music is dehumanizing, the drinks weak, and the clientele dazed. Plus you can't talk. (Maybe that's why most foreigners who have been here for a while prefer to go to or give private parties in order to get together with friends.) Worse, most Tokyo discos enforce a "pairs" code (man-woman couples only; no unaccompanied men), thus sometimes reducing the lone bachelor intent on gaining admission to cruising the entrance, looking for a suitable (or any) woman to accompany him in. But if you take ten or twenty friends with you, almost any entertainment spot can be fun. At any rate, naming the best of this type of entertainment is difficult, even if you like such places, since even a "good" disco becomes repetitive after a few visits. Furthermore, Tokyo discos tend to come and go so fast that by the time this book goes to press, a whole new crop (usually existing, re-designed places) may have sprung up, and some mentioned may have closed. All that said, here are a few you might want to check out:

Contributing to the Ropponganization of Nishi-Azabu is **YELLOW**, a fairly utilitarian place that offers different kinds of music depending on the day of the week: 1st & 3rd Friday: techno; 2nd & 4th Friday: jazz/house; every Saturday: "world color" music; 1st & 3rd Thursdays are gay night, occasional live music, smoky laser effects, etc. Entrance ¥3000 on weekdays; ¥3500 weekends; live music tickets from ¥5000.

1-10-11 Nishi-Azabu. B1-2 Cesaurs Bldg. Tel: 3479-0690. *See Roppongi map.*

JULIANA'S in Shibaura has to be Tokyo's biggest and flashiest place. Absolutely cavernous. Bodysonic floors in places, VIP lounges from which you can get an overview of the action. ¥5000 for men, ¥4500 for women (plus ¥500 on Fri. & Sat.) includes several drinks and snacks.

1-13-10 Shibaura, Chuo-ku. Hours: 6:30 p.m.–midnight. Tel: 5484-4000.

JAVA JIVE, Roppongi. This long-lasting place features a two-level structure in a beach motif with lawn furniture and the like. Thai snacks. Unique here is the reggae/salsa/calypso band that alternates with the recorded disco music. It costs men ¥4000 to get in, women ¥3000, which gets you ten tickets that will buy about four drinks.

Roppongi Square Bldg. B2. 3-10-3 Roppongi, Minato-ku. Hours: 6 p.m.–5 a.m. Tel: 3478-0087. See Roppongi map.

LEXINGTON QUEEN, Roppongi. This is Tokyo's "name" disco, the place that Beautiful People in Roppongi stop you to ask directions to. It's a Tokyo institution, if you will, run by the redoubtable Bill Hersey, a Tokyo institution himself (and busy society columnist for the *Tokyo Weekender*). The place usually finds its way into the itineraries of most visiting luminaries. "Pairs" code rigidly enforced. Unless, of course, you're a celebrity yourself. Even couples containing the requisite number of each sex are not assured entrance to this celebrity-watcher of a club if they happen to be too "crowded" to fit you. Men: ¥4000, women ¥3000 gets you unlimited soft drinks and cocktails.

Daisan Goto Bldg. B1. 3-13-14 Roppongi, Minato-ku. Hours: 6 p.m.–5 a.m. nightly. Tel: 3401-1661. See Roppongi map.

Best Yeah-Yeah-Yeah

The **CAVERN CLUB**, Roppongi. This place does only one thing, and does it well. They offer live Beatles imitators who shake-it-up-baby every night, sometimes using the same model instruments the Fab Four once used. Their sound is authentic, and you can befriend the Japanese Beatles freaks who will no doubt be seated with you at your table. They know all the words and all the harmonies. There's a ¥1300 music charge plus a 20-percent service charge.

Saito Bldg. 1F. 5-3-2 Roppongi, Minato-ku. Hours: 6 p.m.–2:30 a.m., until midnight on Sun. Tel: 3405-5207. See Roppongi map.

Best Live Reggae

HOT CO-ROCKET, Roppongi. Always the best place to dance in Roppongi. Why dance to the latest thumpa-thumpa disco drudge when you can flow with the reggae rhythms done live? The crowd is an interesting mix, and it's easy to meet people here. ¥3000 gets you in and two drinks.

Daini Omasa Bldg. B1. 5-18-2 Roppongi, Minato-ku. Hours: 7 p.m.–3 a.m., Closed Sun. Tel: 3583-9409. *See Roppongi map.*

Best Canned Reggae

CLUB JAMAICA, Nishi-Azabu. With one entire wall of this tiny place taken up by speakers, you probably won't have to worry about being able to hear the music. Actually, you hear more through your vibrating stomach and chest cavity than through your ears. The ¥2500 cover includes two drinks served by a gently swaying bartender. The decor is studiously neglected, bare-bones utilitarian. Understandably, one of Tokyo's best places to meet and mingle with the counterculture. It's a bit hard to find, mainly due to the fact that there is no sign outside, indeed no indication at all that anything is there save for a vague palpitation of the air in the vicinity. From Hobson's at Nishi-Azabu intersection (Kasumicho), go up the hill toward Shibuya. At about the top of this rise, there is a building on the left with a glass door. Club Jamaica is downstairs. Ja, mon.

B1 Ishibashi Bldg. 4-16-14 Nishi-Azabu, Minato-ku. It's only open on Friday and Saturday nights and nights before holidays from 10 p.m.–4 a.m. Tel: 3407-8844. *See Roppongi map.*

Best Glitz

TOKYO TAKARAZUKA GEKIJO, Hibiya. The Takarazuka Revue: lavish, flamboyant, and *c-o-r-n-y*, and not a male in the cast. This troupe sings and dances through romantic, usually Western, musicals (in Japanese) unequaled in their impressive stagecraft. Check out the fans—mostly young teen girls who will wait at the stage door for hours to catch a glimpse of their idols.

1-1-3 Yurakucho, Chiyoda-ku. Tel: 3591-1711. *See Ginza map.*

Best Concert Halls

Highest Tech

SUNTORY HALL, ARK Hills, Roppongi. Incomparable acoustics make this a great place for concerts, especially those featuring soloists. State-of-the-art pipe organ. Although black tie is not required, people do dress up for events here, and the sprinkling of well-designed eating and drinking spots in the ARK Hills complex make for an elegant evening of music plus. You can buy tickets for any visiting performer directly from the hall.

1-13-1 Akasaka, Minato-ku. Tel: 3505-1001. *See Akasaka map.*

Biggest

The 3677-seat **NHK HALL**, adjacent to the NHK Broadcast Center in Shibuya. Japan's Kennedy Center. Also flawless acoustics.

2-2-1 Jinnan, Shibuya-ku. Tel: 3465-1751. *See Shibuya map.*

Best Theater-in-the-Round

GLOBE THEATER. Close to Takadanobaba or Okubo. This high-tech, Japanese version of the Bard's Elizabethan theater has a roof, but its proportions and layout are as authentic as possible. Designed by Arata Isozaki. Catch performances by foreign companies as well as local groups.

3-1-2 Hyakunincho, Shinjuku-ku. Tel: 3360-1121.

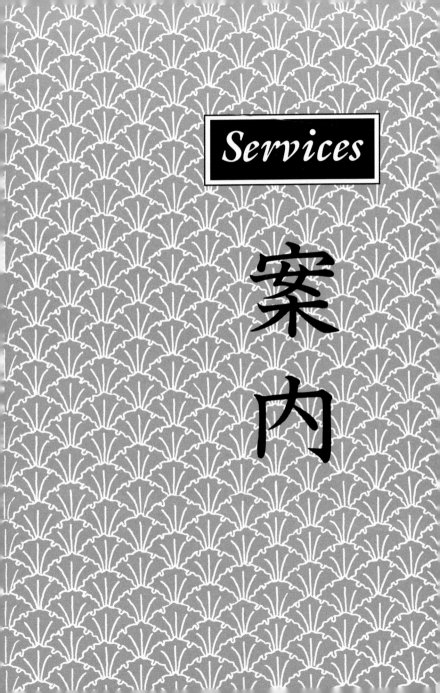

Services

案内

Best Car for Getting Around Tokyo

A TAXI. Do us a favor and slap us around a bit if we ever get the idea into our heads that it would be nice to own a car in this city. You can't even buy one unless you can prove that you have a space to park it at home. And such parking places usually cost as much as apartment rent in saner countries. Taxis here are the most expensive anywhere, but sit back, read your paper, and let someone else fret about the traffic.

Best Taxi

KANEKO TAXI. Tokyo taxis are among the best, cleanest, and most plentiful (and the most expensive) in the world. And the drivers, for the most part polite (they'll even put out their cigarettes if you ask them to), wear white gloves and neckties. But for something completely different, hire this genuine London taxi. That means roomy. The good-natured Tomitaro Kaneko has a phone in the cab to take reservations and enhance his already unique service. People usually reserve the taxi for special occasions, and it's possible to reserve it for a whole day or even for trips.

Car phone: 030-13-23056. *Home phone:* 3402-1061.

Best Rental Equipment

RENTAL SHOP ACOM, Shinjuku. Need a generator to power the sound for your outdoor party? Baseball gear for your team? A VCR or video camera or just about anything else? It's probably available for rent here. Bring

163

your passport or alien registration card for identification when you rent something.

1-34-11 Shinjuku, Shinjuku-ku. Hours: 10 a.m.–7 p.m. daily. Tel: 3350-5081. See Shinjuku map.

Best Phone Information

Finally it's possible to call "information" in English with **NTT'S ENGLISH TELEPHONE INFORMATION SERVICE**. Times are limited, 9 a.m.–5 p.m. weekdays only, and not on holidays. Dial 5295-1010.

Best Map of Tokyo

This is good news: it's **THE FREE ONE AT THE TOURIST INFORMATION CENTER (TIC)**, Yurakucho. Accurate and detailed, this is the best map for getting around town. The helpful TIC also has, of course, numerous pamphlets in English aimed at helping you travel within Japan. There are branches of this information center for non-Japanese-speaking people at Narita airport and in most major cities near central train stations. And they provide free event information in English (3503-2911) and French (3503-2926). They also offer a home visit program, through which you can drop in to a Japanese home for a few hours of conversation over tea and sweets. Go to TIC before noon on the day before you want to visit to enroll.

Kotani Bldg. 1F. 1-6-6 Yurakucho, Chiyoda-ku. Hours: 9 a.m.–5 p.m., until noon on Sat. Closed Sun. & hol. Tel: 3502-1461. See Ginza map.

Best Help for Foreign Shoppers

SEIBU'S FOREIGN CUSTOMER LIAISON OFFICE, Yurakucho, Shibuya, and ARK Hills. You can become a member in this helpful information service by just filling out a form. This done, you'll receive a monthly newsletter in English with information on sales and major events in Tokyo (Seibu also runs the "Ticket Saison" ticket agency).

Yurakucho, A Bldg. 8F. 2-5-1 Yurakucho, Chiyoda-ku. Hours: 10 a.m.–7 p.m. Closed Wed. Tel: 3286-5482. *See Ginza map.*

Seibu Shibuya, B Bldg. 8F. 21-1 Udagawacho, Shibuya-ku. Hours: 10 a.m.–7 p.m. Closed Wed. Tel: 3462-3848. *See Shibuya map.*

Isetan's **I-CLUB**, with a multilingual staff, offers similar services for its customers. They will assign you, at no charge, a "personal shopping assistant" to help you find something your size, often a problem for foreigners here, and they offer free parking and other pluses. Membership in I-Club is also free, and by signing up, you'll be notified about sales, new products, and information on events around Tokyo.

7th floor of the main Isetan building. 14-1-3 Shinjuku, Shinjuku-ku. Hours: 10 a.m.–7 p.m. Closed Wed. Tel: 3225-2515. *See Shinjuku map.*

Best Computer Help

TOKYO UNION CHURCH, Omotesando. Hey, you say, my computer problems aren't *that* bad. But while most computer users believe in an afterlife (probably because most of them have already been through hell), in this one, they merely use TUC's basement for meetings of their users' clubs. You got a problem, you go to the experts. And the experts meet here each month for discussions, problem-sharing/solving, manufacturers' presentations of new products, panel discussions, and the like. The IBM PC Users Club (info: 3576-9783) meets on the 1st Thursday of the month at 7 p.m., and Mac Hackers (info: Francis Barker, 3708-7961) do the same on the last Thursday at around the same time. Call or drop in on a meeting and join up. (Enter through the back door around to the left.) Both groups offer electronic bulletin-board services PC: 3487-9819, Mac: 3708-7971) so you can seek help at any time, and share your expertise and experiences with others. See Aoyama/Harajuku map.

Best Costume Rental

NIHON GEINO BIJUTSU, Shinjuku. Halloween or a costume party coming up? Go as a policeman, a samurai, a (stuffed) sumo wrestler, or in any of a number of disguises. Call in advance and tell them what you want and your size, and your outfit will be ready the next day. Rates run about ¥10,000.

9-15 Wakamatsucho, Shinjuku-ku. Hours: 10 a.m.–6 p.m. Closed 2nd Sat, Sun, & hol. Tel: 3353-2551.

Best Calligraphy Classes

IIJIMA TAKUMA, a member of the executive board of the Japan Calligraphy Association, has performed demonstrations overseas many times, and classes at his home in

Roppongi are very special. The classes are in Japanese, but it's mainly visual learning, and non-verbal communication is a specialty. Classes on Tuesdays and Thursdays.

4-5-7 Roppongi, Minato-ku. Tel: 3401-7983. *See Roppongi map.*

Best Libraries

British

BRITISH COUNCIL. Good selection of reference books, encyclopedias, and some classics.

1-2 Kagurazaka, Shinjuku-ku. Hours: 10 a.m.–9 p.m. Closed Sat., Sun. & hol. Tel: 3235-8031.

American

AMERICAN CENTER. Only Japanese can check out books from here, but anyone can drop by to read.

2-6-3 Shibakoen, Minato-ku. Hours: 10:30 a.m.–6:30 p.m. Closed Sat. & Sun. Tel: 3436-0901.

Japanese

JAPAN FOUNDATION, used mainly by visiting scholars, but outsiders' use possible. About 40,000 books on Japan, half in languages other than Japanese; 80 percent of these are in English. There are also more then 2000 graduate theses from American universities. You can browse by just signing an entrance register, and if you want to borrow, bring your passport (your visa must have two months left on it), and your alien registration card.

Park Bldg. 3F. 3-6 Kioicho, Chiyoda-ku. Hours: 10 a.m.–5 p.m. Closed weekends, last Mon. & hol. Tel: 3263-4504.

The **TOKYO METROPOLITAN CENTRAL LI-BRARY,** adjacent to Arisugawa Park in Hiroo, has 90,000 foreign books.

Hours: Mon.: 1–8 p.m., Tues.–Fri.: 9:30 a.m.–8 p.m. (until 5 p.m. on weekends & hol.) Tel: 3442-8451.

Art History
SUNTORY MUSEUM OF ART

Suntory Bldg. 11F. 1-2-3 Moto-Akasaka, Minato-ku. Hours: 1:30–4 p.m. Wed. & 1:30–3 p.m. Sun. only. Tel: 3470-1073. See Akasaka map.

Sports

運動

Best Two-Wheel Island Trip

MIYAKEJIMA. Just five or six hours away from Tokyo by ferry is this island, still part of the Tokyo Metropolitan Area, which seems to have been made especially for a break from the big city. Board the boat at Takeshiba Pier on Friday evening (sailing time: 10:10 p.m.) after checking your bike, arrive just before 5 a.m., and spend the time until sailing at 1:10 p.m. the next day, Sunday, leisurely touring the island. *Minshuku* (inexpensive inns where dinner and breakfast are usually included in the rate) are numerous. Beaches are clean and uncrowded, and there are beer machines every kilometer or so. See the Tourist Information Center in Yurakucho (3502-1461) for ferry times and lodging information. It's a good idea to reserve your *minshuku* and the ferry tickets in advance, especially during the summer months and on long holiday weekends. Steamship company is Tokai Kisen (3433-1251).

Best Bicycle Exercise Loops

Many think **THE BIG OVAL ROAD ENCIRCLING THE NATIONAL PICTURE GALLERY**, which is closed off to traffic on Sundays, is a good place to get in a few laps on the old ten-speed. And it is. But conditions that make it less than ideal include any nice summer day when bicycles are loaned free of charge to kids, who, as every cyclist knows, ride about as straight as the Mississippi River and do it without looking. So our vote for the best bicycle loop goes to the route **AROUND AKASAKA DETACHED PALACE**. This area borders on Aoyama Dori. Start anywhere and just keep turning left, as the (traffic-free) road winds up and down tree-lined streets and around the palace. Lovely.

Best Martial Arts Info

If you're here to study martial arts, here are the places you can start looking for lessons and information:

Karate

NIHON KARATE KYOKAI. Class hours: 4–8 p.m. except Sun. & hol. Many foreigners are taking classes here, and only a little Japanese language is needed. Just

¥20,000 gets you started. That includes the initiation fee of ¥10,000, the first month's dues of ¥7000, and the yearly fee of ¥3000.

1-6-1 Ebisu Nishi, Shibuya-ku. Tel: 3462-1415.

Judo

KODOKAN. Practice sessions or observation. The All-Japan Judo Federation office is in the same place. The people there can tell you which *dojo* is nearest you.

1-16-30 Kasuga, Bunkyo-ku. Tel: 3811-7151.

Aikido

AIKIKAI HOMBU DOJO. Hours: 6:30 a.m.–8 p.m. daily. Beginning and mixed classes. Run by the son of the founder of aikido. Instructors are direct disciples of the founder, Morihei Ueshiba.

17-18 Wakamatsucho, Shinjuku-ku. Tel: 3203-9236.

Kyudo (archery)

MEIJI JINGU KYUDO-JO, called *Iseikan*. Located in Meiji Jingu compound. Take lessons or watch. Hours: 5–8 p.m. Mon., Tues., Thurs. Registration: ¥2000. Monthly dues: ¥3000.

1-1 Kamizonocho, Yoyogi, Shibuya-ku. Tel: 3379-5511.

Kendo

KYUMEIKAN DOJO. Hours: 7–9 p.m. Mon., Wed., Fri. Registration fee: ¥10,000. Monthly dues: ¥5000. Aimed at Japanese students but they will explain what they're doing in English.

2-1-7 Akatsuka Shinmachi, Itabashi-ku. Tel: 3930-4636.

Best Fitness Club

Tokyo has a wealth of fitness clubs, ranging from the very affordable, usually operated by your ward, to the ludicrously expensive. The best one is the one nearest your work or home, and is therefore **THE ONE YOU WILL USE REGULARLY**.

Best All-Day Sports Sucker

A sumo match at **RYOGOKU KOKUGIKAN**, just north of Ryogoku Station. Bench seats up in the back cost ¥1500, box seats (which include lunch and saké) cost ¥8000–¥10,000. Second-level seats are ¥2300–¥7000. Since the box seats are well nigh impossible to get, we recommend the bench seats and a pair of binoculars. Bouts start at noon, but the biggies generally bump heads from 5–6 p.m. There's a museum on the premises depicting the sport's 2000-year history. Three of the six yearly sumo tournaments are held here, in January, May, and September. They usually start on the second Sunday of the month and last 15 days. The entire Ryogoku area is riddled with sumo-related shops.

1-3-28 Yokoami, Sumida-ku. Tel: 3623-5111.

Best Jogging Routes

AROUND THE IMPERIAL PALACE has always been a popular circuit for joggers who live within running distance, and it's probably the best. It offers ever-changing views to enjoy through the sweat. Also good is the track **AROUND THE NHK BROADCAST CENTER**

in Shibuya. Starting at the south entrance to the complex, the track circles the Center as well as the two Olympic stadiums.

Best Baseball Team

THE EAGLES. Well, maybe the Lions or the Giants, or even the Carp are better, but they probably won't let you play with them. The Eagles, organized by the irrepressible Osamu Kato, are an all-*gaijin* team (it's open to Japanese players, but for some reason none have signed up) that plays factory and city teams in the Gaien League. Twelve Japanese teams are met each year, teams with names like the Drunkards and the Crazies. It costs ¥20,000 per year to play, and the idea, of course, is to compete, perchance to win, and afterward to engage in uplifting cultural exchanges (read: drinking) with the opposing teams. Call Kato at 0425-36-8354 for information on how to join.

Best Swimming Pools

Outdoor

JINGU POOL near Sendagaya Station is a 50-meter pool bordered by a stepped, green-carpeted, grandstand-type area for sunning or people-watching. Most people go home at 6 p.m., but in summer it's open until 9, creating a nice, uncrowded interval for you. Another plus is that little kids who have yet to prove that they can swim a required 50 meters must stay in the adjacent indoor pool. It's open from mid-June to mid-October. Cost: ¥1,500. In the winter it becomes an ice skating rink (10 a.m.–7 p.m., ¥1200).

5 Kasumigaoka, Shinjuku-ku. Hours: 10 a.m.–6 p.m. (9:30 a.m.–9 p.m. between mid-July and August 31st). Tel: 3403-3458.

Indoor

Located right in front of Sendagaya Station on the Sobu Line, **SENDAGAYA GYMNASIUM & SWIMMING POOL** is a huge compound operated by the City of Tokyo. The main, enclosed, stadium is often the venue for world-class sports competitions, and next to it are the running course, gym, and swimming pools. There are a 25-meter and a 50-meter pool, the latter is often used for international competitions. The high ceilings and large windows at the 50-meter pool make for a relaxing atmosphere, and the floors are heated, so you can lie down at poolside even in winter. Since it's run by the city government, there are, however, some strict rules that must be followed. Like everyone out of the pool for 10 minutes every hour. And lots of prison . . . uh . . . lifeguards keep close tabs on you to make sure you don't drown or do something really bad, like forget your swimming cap or not shower before entering the water or not stay in your lane. No soap or shampoo is allowed in the shower rooms. Obviously, this place is only for those who are serious about swimming. It's open from 9 a.m. until 8:30 p.m., and to avoid the crowds, go at 8 and have the place almost to yourself, since most people leave at about that time. The upside is that it's only ¥400, with a two-hour limit during the summer. Check the pool schedule in advance, since it is closed to the public when competitions are under way. Tel: 5474-2111

The pool at the **HOTEL OKURA** offers special summer memberships for non-guests. Mid-June to mid-September: ¥80,000. Members can swim any time the pool is open, usually 8 a.m.– 9 p.m., but times vary depending on the month. Or perhaps the ¥40,000 deal, for swimming after 3:30 p.m. only, would suit you better.

2-10-4 Toranomon, Minato-ku. Tel: 3582-0111. *See Akasaka map.*

Best Ski Weekends

Skiing approaches mania status in Japan, with hundreds of resorts to check out. But for the foreigner, arranging transportation, lodging, meals, lift tickets, etc., can be somewhat daunting. Let the **SHIN-YI SKI CLUB** figure it all out for you. In operation for more than 20 years, they plan at least eight weekend trips a year, all-inclusive, for ¥35,000–¥45,000. That includes transportation, lodging, breakfasts, and Saturday dinner. Ski rental, lift tickets, beverages, and any other costs are paid directly by the skier. Shin-YI welcomes skiers of all levels, and will help beginners select rental equipment and get started. The group is truly international, with members from a dozen countries. Call Godfrey Bull, who runs the club, to get started.

33 Shinanomachi Mansion, 4-20 Minamimotocho, Shinjuku-ku 160. Tel: 3353-6835. Fax: 3225-4869.

Miscellaneous

其他

Best Stand-Up-for-Your-Rights Izakaya

TAMAKYU, Shibuya. Notice how the futuristic 109 Building on Dogenzaka in Shibuya has to allow for a scruffy little wooden building on one side? That's Tamakyu, a long-time eatery that wouldn't sell out to the big developers. The specialty is grilled fish, and it is truly wonderful here, along with the appropriate saké. Tamakyu has gained a reputation for being choosy about its customers, a fact which some foreigners have taken personally. But relax. It also frightens away some of the sillier Shibuya college-kid/salaryman types that they do not think will pay their wonderful food the proper respect. Hey, you don't take on an economic giant like Tokyu— and win—only to allow your place to fall prey to loud, sloppy drinkers. No, it's only for people who appreciate what magic can be done with a humble fish. Appreciate the food and they will appreciate you, even welcome you back.

2-30-4 Dogenzaka, Shibuya-ku. Hours: 4–11 p.m. Closed Sun. & hol. Tel: 3461-4803. *See Shibuya map.*

Best Neighborhood Festival

AZABU JUBAN. Azabu Juban in Minato-ku probably has a higher percentage of foreign residents than any other part of town, so its summer *O-bon* festival tends to be more on the lines of a mini-world's fair. At the bottom of the *shotengai* (shopping street) and across the big street, under the three elevated expressways, members of foreign communities as disparate as Korean, Iranian, and

181

British get together to set up stalls where everything from beer and food to clothing is sold. And then there's the manic Keio University Brazilian Drum Band, made up of about a hundred rhythm-makers, who snake their way through the area. Late August, from around 4–9:30. Check the August "Festivals" section in Tokyo Journal. There's also *bon-odori* dancing, with drums and all, and foreigners seriously wanting to try will be welcomed. It's not hard. See Roppongi map.

Best Yurt

Yes, yurt. The tent-like structures of Mongolia. **PAO**, in Nakano, is definitely a unique dining experience, if not exactly for the food. You sit inside a genuine yurt, dismantled and reassembled here, on a bed of carpets by a circular fire pit while quaffing Chinese wine and snacking on a variety of what they call here "ethnic" foods, whatever that means. The tent is open to the sky, which could be a problem in a storm, but the laid-back staff doesn't seem to be concerned.

2-25-6 Higashi Nakano, Nakano-ku. Hours: 11:30 a.m.–5 p.m., 6 p.m.–midnight. Closed Tues. Tel: 3371-3750.

Best Place to Study Japanese Crafts

JAPAN TRADITIONAL CRAFTS CENTER. Many different kinds of Japanese crafts are represented here. And there are a number of videos, some in English, depicting traditional craftsmen at work—making *washi* (paper), cloth dyeing, etc. Some of the videos are about the work and lives of Japan's Living National Treasures (that is, master craftsmen). There's an exhibition space, and crafts are offered for sale as well. Demonstrations are sometimes given. Call for details.

Plaza 246 2F. 3-1-1 Minami-Aoyama, Minato-ku. Hours: 10 a.m.–6 p.m. Closed Thurs. Tel: 3403-2460. *See Aoyama/ Harajuku map.*

Best Feature to Include In Your New VCR

We don't usually hawk Japanese electronic goodies in these books, but our new VCR has an astounding new feature that we thought you ought to know about, since it is advertised only sparingly for obvious reasons. It's Mitsubishi's **COMMERCIAL ELIMINATOR** that, as you record, puts the VCR on pause when the commercials come on. Makes all the movies you record seem like they were broadcast on commercial-free NHK or WOWOW. It doesn't get any better than this. Only works on bilingual movies. Now if they can invent a gadget that will correct all the seemingly indiscriminate slicing they do to make all movies exactly an hour and 47 minutes long. . . .

Best Western TV News

CBS EVENING NEWS. (If you've got cable TV or a satellite receiver, ignore the following, but others read on.) Sure, there are bilingual translations of Japanese TV news programs here, but unless you're obsessively interested in tax debate, the northern islands dispute, education reform, and all those other edge-of-the-seat issues, it does little good to watch something just because it's in English. Better, more international news fare can be had for just a little effort. Tokyo Broadcasting System (TBS, Ch. 6) broadcasts The CBS Evening News with Dan Rather five days a week (at 5:10 a.m. at this writing, but check the dailies, as this has changed throughout the years). That's a bit early for Dan, we admit, but with a VCR and timer, you can tape it and catch up on the news of the world when you like. Channel 6 also airs some 60 Minutes and 48 Hours segments in their **CBS DOCU-MENTARIES**, just after midnight on Sunday nights.

Locally produced and somewhat less polished, but still heavy on the international news with many satellite film clips from Britain, America, and other countries is **THE WORLD TODAY**, on JCTV (Japan Cable Television) at 7 p.m., Monday through Friday. It's rebroadcast on KTV in Yokohama (Ch. 42, UHF) at 11:30 p.m. You can pick up a little antenna-lead divider for about ¥1000 that allows you to make use of your TV's UHF capabilities.

Best Free Smorgasbord

THE BASEMENT OF JUST ABOUT ANY MAJOR DEPARTMENT STORE, where hundreds of kinds of food are on the block, most available for sampling. It's a great and quick way to learn what the Japanese eat. Should you find something you like and develop a taste for it, be reminded that discounts are always available on days before the store takes its weekly day off and holidays. The basements of Seibu (Shibuya and Yurakucho) and Isetan (Shinjuku) are particularly good, although Mitsukoshi (Ginza) has more traditional Japanese fare.

Best Boat Trips

Two boat rental companies operate most of the boats on the scenic Sumida. **KOMATSUYA** (Tel: 3851-2780) rents out traditional-style boats made of *hinoki*, Japanese cypress. The charge is ¥15,000 per person (groups of more than 10 people) and includes tempura (they stress that it's the freshest; they never use frozen) and some

snacks. The charge does not include drinks, but you can bring your own. **AMISEI** (Tel: 3844-1869) offers more modern boats able to set sail with up to 100 people. Tatami mats are standard, and although headroom varies, a few boats have the foot wells so welcome to foreigners. Amisei charges ¥10,000 per person (minimum 20 people), which includes beer, saké, juice, tempura, sashimi and snacks. Some boats even have tables and chairs. The boats carry karaoke (sing-along) sets, but foreigners may want to hire a *shamisen* player to provide the mood music instead. It's kind of nice floating along off Hamarikyu Garden with the Tokyo skyline in full splendor, listening to the soothing music. If a traditional boat trip is not to your liking, the **SUIJO BUS** (water bus) is a far cheaper way to get out on the river. It plies the waves from Azumabashi, the bridge near Asakusa Station, to Hinode Pier in Hamamatsucho. The 40-minute trip costs ¥560. Tel: 3841-9178 (Asakusa) or 3457-7830 (Hinode Pier), in Japanese.

In recent years other boat excursions have sprung up, and now you have your choice of about 10 cruises to take. All these boats are new and very clean, some as big as three decks, and all very spacious, some with open decks and wide windows. You can go to the Museum of Maritime Science via Odaiba out in the middle of the bay, or to Kasai Rinkai Koen, a park opened a few years ago and popular for its aquarium and man-made beach. From there you can change to another boat for Edogawa. And then we have what are called "restaurant boats" and their sunset cruises. You can be served either Western, Japanese or grilled seafood and veggies for about ¥7800, which includes the meal, drinks, and taxes. These sunset cruises usually leave at around 6:30 and take about two hours. Call 3433-5591 for information.

Best Magic Bus

Not many foreigners would consider riding around in Tokyo traffic to be much fun, but, as they do in so many things, the Japanese have a different idea of what makes a good time. And we must admit, if you let someone else do the driving and take 20 or 30 friends and some food and drink along, the whole experience can take on a different aspect. You can rent an entire bus to take your party to its destination, or, lacking one of those, just to cruise around the supercity and enjoy the company and the scenery. You can determine your own route, of course. **HATO BUS** (3201-1313), the company operating those yellow tour buses with a *hato* (dove) on the side, will rent you one of their 50-seat coaches from 10 a.m. to sundown for about ¥100,000–¥150,000, and you must bring your own food and drink. A luxurious alternative is one of the "salon cars" operated by **KM KANKO** (3201-0111). These rolling palaces come equipped with electronics—tapes, CDs, video, and of course the ubiquitous karaoke—as well as microwave ovens and the hard-to-escape crystal chandelier. A group no smaller than 15 can rent this kitsch carriage for three hours after 5 p.m. for approximately ¥7000 per person. Approximately because the price is flexible, allowing you to tailor your bus ride to whatever you have in mind.

Best Fireworks

The fireworks (*hanabi*) over the Sumida River in Asakusa have been held annually for more than 350 years, and they are truly awe-inspiring. If, that is, you can get near them. For their fame has made them somewhat of a bother to get to. A million people flood the already packed neighborhood, and it can take hours just to get out of the place after the pyrotechnics are over. (If you do go to this show, by the way, buy your return train ticket on your arrival to speed your exit.) But the little-known fact is that the display over the **ARAKAWA RIVER** at Kita-Senju a few days later is nearly as elaborate and a whole lot easier to get to and away from. You can sit on a grassy levee practically under the fireworks and hear every pop and sizzle. It's conveniently located near Kita-Senju Station on the Hibiya and Chiyoda lines. Just follow the crowds to the riverbank and bring a picnic and a few beers. It happens in late July. You can get a different angle on all these pyrotechnics by hopping on a boat and watching from there. The *Shitamachi Times,* a newspaper especially for this old downtown area, organizes boat trips every year to both the Sumida and the Arakawa River fireworks. The trip costs about ¥10,000 per person and includes a meal and some drinks. Call 3634-4721 in Japanese.

Best People-Watching

CAFÉ de ROPÉ, Harajuku. Once the top place for the frivolity described above, its service got too good and it was eclipsed by the nearby B-Haus. But when that place turned into a Haagen Dazs, Ropé regained its title. A place for purist people-watchers and lovers of good coffee.

6-1-8 Jingumae, Shibuya-ku. Hours: 11 a.m.–11 p.m. daily. Tel: 3406-6845. *See Aoyama/Harajuku map.*

Best Geisha-Watching

AKASAKA KAIKAN, in the heart of one of the oldest traditional eating, drinking, and being-merry neighborhoods in the city. This is a place where *geisha* go many afternoons to practice their *tsutsumi*, *shamisen*, and other cultural talents. Many dress for work there and board one of the *riksha* parked out front to be taken to their assigned parties. See Akasaka map.

Best So-Bad-It's-Good Film About Japan

KARATE KID II. Dumb even to people who don't live in Japan, this film is a classic crack-up to anyone who has been in Japan even for just a little while. It takes place in a fishing village in Okinawa, but, failing to find a suitable site in Okinawa, the producers built one—in Hawaii. All the villagers trundle through the unpaved streets with televisions in wheelbarrows and speak a charming pidgin English. The baddies drive black '68 Cadillacs, and a *bon-odori* dance takes on the atmosphere of a voodoo rite. Rent it for a guaranteed hilarious video party.

Best Festivals

Biggest annual

SANJA MATSURI, Asakusa. One of the biggest and most crowded Edokko (hearty common folk of Tokyo) festivals, and a great example of the Japanese working together to support several one-ton shrines all day. Ritual dances and music, too. Third Saturday and Sunday of May; follow the crowds from Asakusa Station.

Wettest

TOMIOKA HACHIMANGU FUKAGAWA MATSU-RI. A parade of *mikoshi* at which parade watchers continually douse the hard-working carriers of these portable (by 50 people) shrines as they go by. It happens in the hot month of August, so the cool water is quite welcome. Near Monzen-Nakacho on the Tozai Line. Once every three years: 1995, 1998, 2001, etc.

Best Toilet

Okay, there had to be one, and entrants were judged solely on originality. It's in **ICHIOKU**, the eclectic restaurant already mentioned in the "Eating" section of this book. You have to see this room to believe it. The mirror is framed in an old TV set; the commode, Japanese style, is a rock garden; a tasteless velvet painting of an old Chinese man has a peephole in one of its eyes. And to make your comfort complete, a 50s-vintage clock radio is constantly tuned to FEN. Enjoy yourself.

4-4-5 Roppongi, Minato-ku. Hours: 5:30 p.m.–12:30 a.m. daily. Tel: 405-9891. *See Roppongi map.*

Runners-up are the john at the Meguro Gajoen wedding palace, with its rivers, bridges and foilage, and the absolutely relaxing one at the Canadian Embassy, 4th floor.

Best Visual Aid

You usually remember **BINOCULARS** just as you sit down at a concert. We've done the shopping for you and sampled all the types of binoculars available. The verdict: Nikon's 7 x 21, 7.1 are the ones to own. That means seven times magnification, 21 mm objective lenses, and a 7.1-degree field of view (ain't we technical?), yet small and light enough to carry around in your shoulder bag or purse, these little things produce a high-quality image and are easy to use. Indispensable for concerts and sports, great for travel and nature outings. About ¥10,000 to ¥12,000, depending on where you buy and how good your bargaining skills are.

Maps

地図

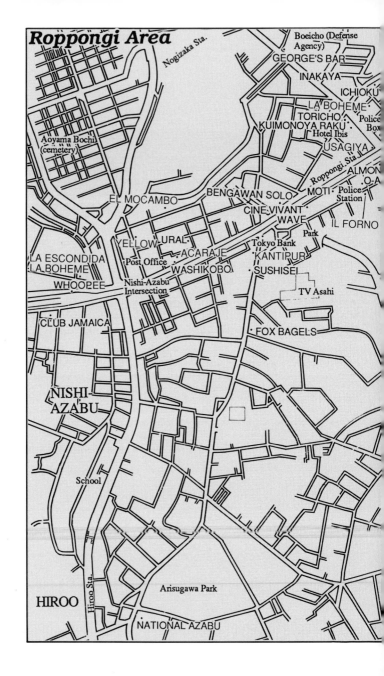

Roppongi Area

Nogizaka Sta.

Boeicho (Defense Agency)

GEORGE'S BAR

INAKAYA

ICHIOKU

LA BOHEME

TORICHO

KUIMONOYA RAKU

Police Box

Hotel Ibis

USAGIYA

Aoyama Bochi (cemetery)

Roppongi Sta.

ALMON

O-A

EL MOCAMBO

BENGAWAN SOLO

MOTI

Police Station

CINE VIVANT

WAVE

IL FORNO

Park

YELLOW URAL

ACARAJE

Tokyo Bank

KANTIPUR

LA ESCONDIDA

LA BOHEME

Post Office

WASHIKOBO

SUSHISEI

WHOOPEE

Nishi-Azabu Intersection

TV Asahi

CLUB JAMAICA

FOX BAGELS

NISHI-AZABU

School

HIROO

Hiroo Sta.

Arisugawa Park

NATIONAL AZABU

194

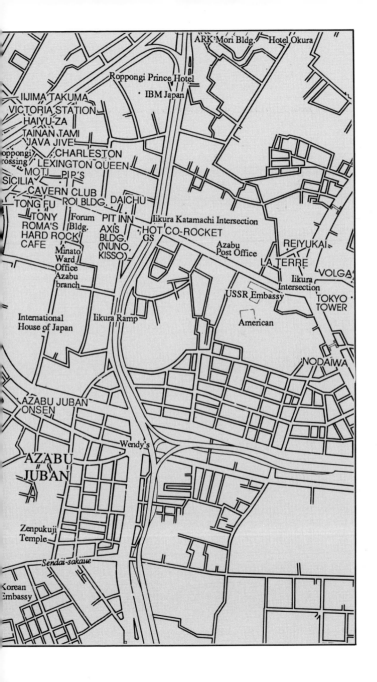

ARK Mori Bldg.   Hotel Okura

Roppongi Prince Hotel

• IBM Japan

IIJIMA TAKUMA
VICTORIA STATION
HAIYU-ZA
TAINAN TAMI
JAVA JIVE
oppongi   CHARLESTON
rossing   LEXINGTON QUEEN
MOTI   PIP'S
SICILIA
CAVERN CLUB
TONG FU   ROI BLDG.   DAICHU
TONY   PIT INN   Iikura Katamachi Intersection
ROMA'S   Forum   AXIS   HOT CO-ROCKET
HARD ROCK Bldg.   BLDG. GS   Azabu
CAFE   (NUNO.   Post Office   REIYUKAI
      Minato   KISSO)   LA TERRE
      Ward   VOLGA
      Office   Iikura
      Azabu   Intersection
      branch   TOKYO
                              USSR Embassy   TOWER
International   American
House of Japan   Iikura Ramp
                                                          NODAIWA

AZABU JUBAN
ONSEN

AZABU   Wendy's
JUBAN

Zenpukuji
Temple
      Sendai-sakaue

Korean
Embassy

195

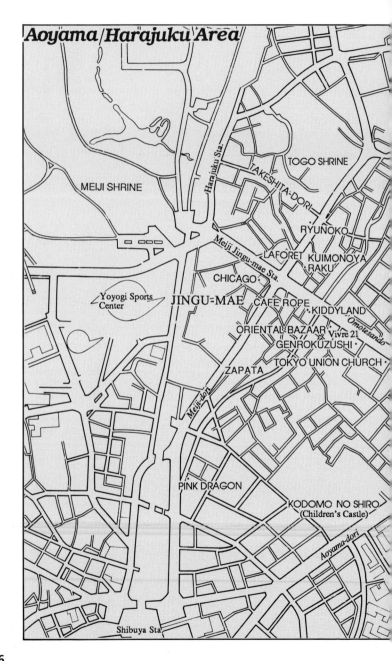

Aoyama/Harajuku Area

MEIJI SHRINE

Harajuku Sta.

TOGO SHRINE

TAKESHITA-DORI

RYUNOKO

Meiji Jingu-mae Sta.

LAFORET

KUIMONOYA

RAKU

CHICAGO

Yoyogi Sports Center

JINGU=MAE

CAFE ROPE

KIDDYLAND

ORIENTAL BAZAAR

Vivre 21

Omotesando

GENROKUZUSHI

TOKYO UNION CHURCH

ZAPATA

Meiji-dori

PINK DRAGON

KODOMO NO SHIRO
(Children's Castle)

Aoyama-dori

Shibuya Sta.

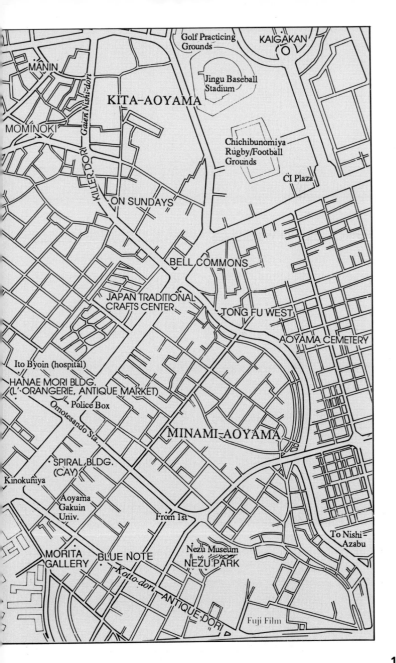

KAIGAKAN

Golf Practicing
Grounds

Jingu Baseball
Stadium

MANIN

KITA-AOYAMA

MOMINOKI

Chichibunomiya
Rugby/Football
Grounds

CI Plaza

ON SUNDAYS

BELL COMMONS

JAPAN TRADITIONAL
CRAFTS CENTER

TONG FU WEST

AOYAMA CEMETERY

Ito Byoin (hospital)

HANAE MORI BLDG.
(L'·ORANGERIE, ANTIQUE MARKET)

Police Box

Omotesando Sta.

MINAMI-AOYAMA

SPIRAL BLDG.
(CAY)

Kinokuniya

Aoyama
Gakuin
Univ.

From 1st

To Nishi-
Azabu

MORITA
GALLERY

BLUE NOTE

Nezu Museum
NEZU PARK

Kotto-dori

ANTIQUE DORI

Fuji Film

197

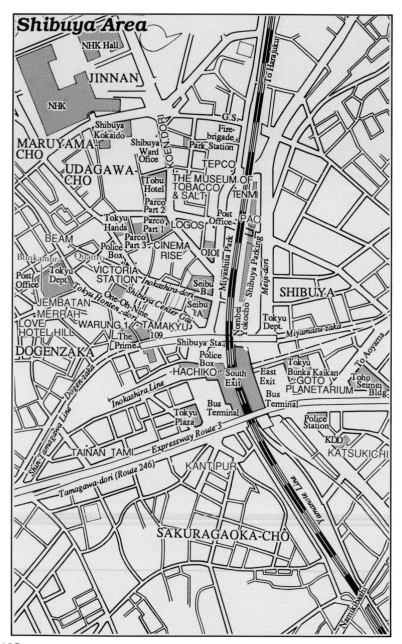

Shibuya Area

NHK Hall

JINNAN

NHK

MARUYAMA-CHO

Shibuya Kokaido

Shibuya Ward Office

UDAGAWA-CHO

KOEN-DORI

G.S.

Fire-brigade

Park Station

TEPCO

Tobu Hotel

THE MUSEUM OF TOBACCO & SALT

TENMI

Parco Part 2

Parco Part 1

Tokyu Hands

Post Office

PAO

BEAM

Parco Part 3

LOGOS

CINEMA RISE

OIOI

Bunkamura

Quattro

Police Box

VICTORIA STATION

Miyashita Park

Shibuya Parking

Meiji-dori

SHIBUYA

Post Office

Tokyu Dept.

Inokashira-dori

Seibu B.

JEMBATAN

One-Oh-Nine

Shibuya Center Gai

Seibu A.

Tokyu Honten-dori

MERRAH

LOVE HOTEL HILL

WARUNG 1

TAMAKYU

Nombei Yokocho

Tokyu Dept.

DOGENZAKA

The Prime

109

Shibuya Sta.

Miyamasu-zaka

Police Box

HACHIKO

South Exit

East Exit

Tokyu Bunka Kaikan

To Aoyama

GOTO PLANETARIUM

Toho Seimei Bldg.

Dogen-zaka

Inokashira Line

Bus Terminal

Bus Terminal

Police Station

Shin-Tamagawa Line

Tokyu Plaza

KDD

KATSUKICHI

TAINAN TAMI

Expressway Route 3

KANTIPUR

Tamagawa-dori (Route 246)

Yamanote Line

SAKURAGAOKA-CHO

Namikibashi

To Harajuku

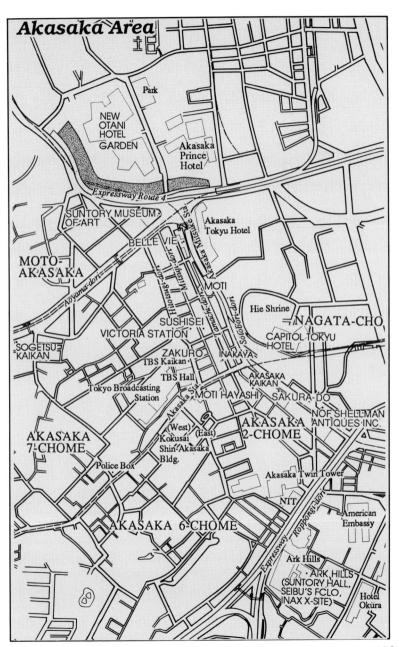

Akasaka Area

Park

NEW OTANI HOTEL GARDEN

Akasaka Prince Hotel

Expressway Route 4

SUNTORY MUSEUM OF ART

BELLE VIE

Akasaka Tokyu Hotel

Akasaka Mitsuke Sta.

MOTO-AKASAKA

Aoyama-dori

Hitotsugi-dori

Mitsuke-dori

MOTI

Tamachi-dori

Sotobori-dori

Hie Shrine

NAGATA-CHO

SUSHISEI

VICTORIA STATION

CAPITOL TOKYU HOTEL

SOGETSU KAIKAN

ZAKURO

TBS Kaikan

INAKAYA

TBS Hall

AKASAKA KAIKAN

Tokyo Broadcasting Station

Akasaka Sta.

MOTI HAYASHI

SAKURA-DO

N.OF SHELLMAN ANTIQUES INC.

(West)

(East)

AKASAKA 2-CHOME

AKASAKA 7-CHOME

Kokusai Shin-Akasaka Bldg.

Police Box

Akasaka Twin Tower

NTT

American Embassy

AKASAKA 6-CHOME

Roppongi-dori

Expressway

Ark Hills

ARK HILLS (SUNTORY HALL, SEIBU'S FCLO, INAX X-SITE)

Hotel Okura

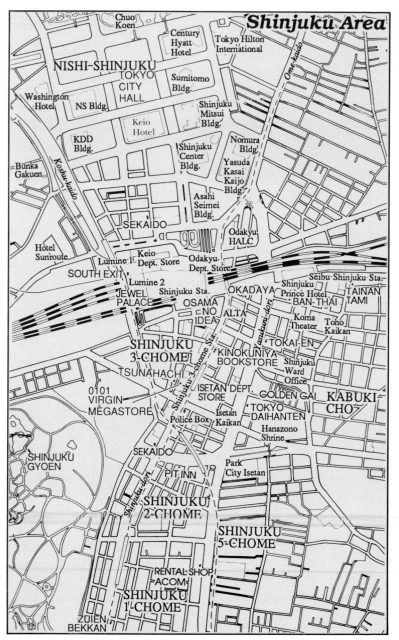

Shinjuku Area

Chuo
Koen

Century
Hyatt
Hotel

Tokyo Hilton
International

Ome-kaido

NISHI-SHINJUKU

TOKYO
CITY
HALL

Sumitomo
Bldg.

Washington
Hotel

NS Bldg.

Shinjuku
Mitsui
Bldg.

Koshu-kaido

Keio
Hotel

KDD
Bldg.

Shinjuku
Center
Bldg.

Nomura
Bldg.

Yasuda
Kasai
Kaijo
Bldg.

Bunka
Gakuen

SEKAIDO

Asahi
Seimei
Bldg.

Odakyu
HALC

Hotel
Sunroute

Keio
Dept. Store

Odakyu
Dept. Store

Lumine

SOUTH EXIT

Lumine 2

Seibu-Shinjuku-Sta.

JEWEL
PALACE

Shinjuku Sta.

OKADAYA

Shinjuku
Prince Hotel

BAN-THAI

TAINAN
TAMI

OSAMA

ALTA

Koma
Theater

Toho
Kaikan

NO
IDEA

TOKAI-EN

SHINJUKU
3-CHOME

KINOKUNIYA
BOOKSTORE

Shinjuku
Ward
Office

TSUNAHACHI

ISETAN DEPT.
STORE

0101
VIRGIN
MEGASTORE

GOLDEN GAI

KABUKI
CHO

TOKYO
DAIHANTEN

Police Box

Isetan
Kaikan

Hanazono
Shrine

SHINJUKU
GYOEN

SEKAIDO

Park
City Isetan

PIT INN

SHINJUKU
2-CHOME

SHINJUKU
5-CHOME

Shinjuku-dori

RENTAL SHOP
ACOM

SHINJUKU
1-CHOME

ZUIEN
BEKKAN

200

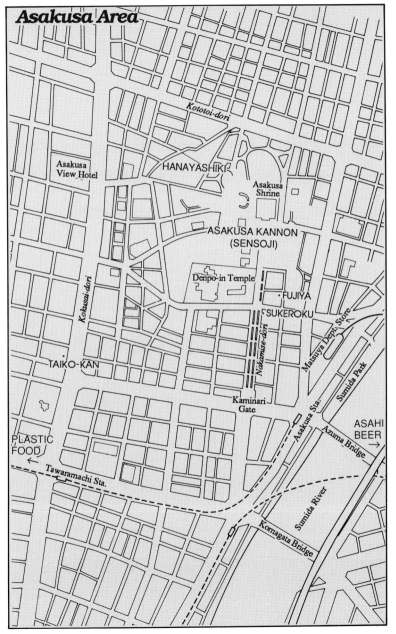

Asakusa Area

Kototoi-dori

Asakusa View Hotel

HANAYASHIKI

Asakusa Shrine

ASAKUSA KANNON (SENSOJI)

Kokusai-dori

Denpo-in Temple

· FUJIYA

SUKEROKU

Matsuya Dept. Store

Nakamise-dori

Sumida Park

TAIKO-KAN

Kaminari Gate

Asakusa Sta.

ASAHI BEER →

PLASTIC FOOD

Azuma Bridge

Tawaramachi Sta.

Sumida River

Komagata Bridge

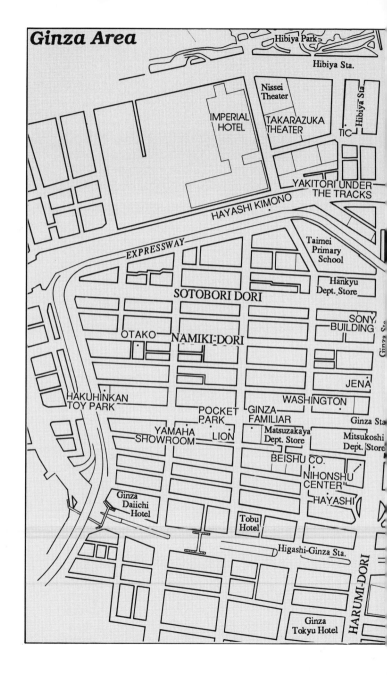

Ginza Area

Hibiya Park
Hibiya Sta.
Hibiya Sta.

Nissei Theater
IMPERIAL HOTEL
TAKARAZUKA THEATER
TIC

YAKITORI UNDER THE TRACKS

HAYASHI KIMONO

EXPRESSWAY

Taimei Primary School

Hankyu Dept. Store

SOTOBORI DORI

SONY BUILDING

Ginza Sta

OTAKO
NAMIKI-DORI

JENA

WASHINGTON

HAKUHINKAN TOY PARK

POCKET PARK
GINZA FAMILIAR

Ginza Sta

YAMAHA SHOWROOM
LION
Matsuzakaya Dept. Store

Mitsukoshi Dept. Store

BEISHU CO.

NIHONSHU CENTER

HAYASHI

Ginza Daiichi Hotel

Tobu Hotel

Higashi-Ginza Sta.

HARUMI-DORI

Ginza Tokyu Hotel

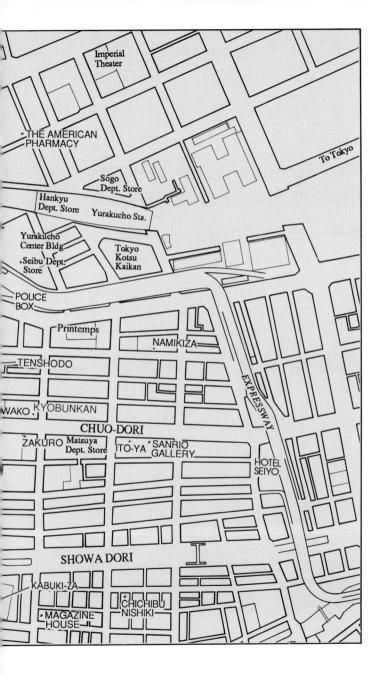

Imperial
Theater

THE AMERICAN
PHARMACY

Sōgo
Dept. Store

Hankyu
Dept. Store

Yurakucho Sta.

To Tokyo

Yurakucho
Center Bldg.

Seibu Dept.
Store

Tokyo
Kotsu
Kaikan

POLICE
BOX

Printemps

NAMIKIZA

TENSHODO

EXPRESSWAY

WAKO KYOBUNKAN

CHUO-DORI

ZAKURO Matsuya
Dept. Store

ITO-YA

SANRIO
GALLERY

HOTEL
SEIYO

SHOWA DORI

KABUKI-ZA

CHICHIBU
NISHIKI

MAGAZINE
HOUSE

203

Index

OTHER TUTTLE BOOKS
OF INTEREST

OLD TOKYO
Walks in the City of the Shogun
Sumiko Enbutsu

A fun and informative walking guide from the author of *Chichibu* that takes the reader through Tokyo's past, revealing hidden pockets of history and culture.

CHICHIBU
Japan's Hidden Treasure
Sumiko Enbutsu

The rich legacy of Chichibu's folklore and traditions are retold in this indispensable text. A guide to the famous circuit of 34 *kannon* temples is included.

TUTTLE'S ILLUSTRATED
GUIDE TO JAPAN
Alan Booth, photographs by Ken Straiton

This detailed travel guide by the author of *The Roads to Sata* includes 49 color photos and 12 maps covering every part of Japan.

JAPAN
An Invitation
Ray Furse

A comprehensive single-volume introduction to Japan with over 130 color photos taken by leading photographers.

JAPAN
The Art of Living
Amy S. Katoh, photographs by Shin Kimura

This handsome book introduces Japanache, a new style of living that harmoniously blends East and West, traditional and modern.

NIPPON
Land of Beauty and Tradition
Philip Sandoz, photographs by Narumi Yasuda

This impressive volume takes the reader on a kaleidescopic tour of Japan's fascinating regions.

KABUKI
A Pocket Guide
Ronald Cavaye

This informative text explains Kabuki theater as it is performed today. Highly readable, it will be of interest to fans of all levels.

JAPANESE FESTIVALS
Helen Bauer and Sherwin Carlquist

This indispensable guide lists 355 annual festivals in Japan along with timetables and locations.

TOKYO NIGHT CITY
Where to Drink and Party After Hours
Jude Brand

This book maps the maze of Tokyo's drinking, mingling, and dancing spots from the easy hours after sundown to the frontier hours after the sun comes up.

TOKYO SIGHTS AND INSIGHTS
Ryosuke Kami

This guide takes a look at 88 interesting sights of traditional Tokyo.

TOKYO MUSEUM GUIDE
Tom and Ellen Flannigan

An exhaustive guide to all the museums in the Tokyo and Yokohama metropolitan area.